Selected Papers From the Fifth World Congress of Central and East European Studies, Warsaw, 1995

Edited for the International Council for Central and East European Studies by **Ronald J. Hill**, Professor of Comparative Government, Trinity College, University of Dublin, Ireland

Titles include:

Todd Patrick Armstrong (*editor*)
PERSPECTIVES ON MODERN CENTRAL AND EAST EUROPEAN LITERATURE
Quests for Identity

Sue Bridger (*editor*)
WOMEN AND POLITICAL CHANGE
Perspectives from East-Central Europe

J. A. Dunn (*editor*)
LANGUAGE AND SOCIETY IN POST-COMMUNIST EUROPE

William E. Ferry and Roger E. Kanet (*editors*)
POST-COMMUNIST STATES IN THE WORLD COMMUNITY

Graeme Gill (*editor*)
ELITES AND LEADERSHIP IN RUSSIAN POLITICS

Paul G. Hare (*editor*)
SYSTEMIC CHANGE IN POST-COMMUNIST ECONOMIES

A. Kemp-Welch (*editor*)
STALINISM IN POLAND, 1944–56

Stanislav J. Kirschbaum (*editor*)
HISTORICAL REFLECTIONS ON CENTRAL EUROPE

Carol S. Leonard (*editor*)
THE MICROECONOMICS OF POST-COMMUNIST CHANGE

Kevin McDermott and John Morison (*editors*)
POLITICS AND SOCIETY UNDER THE BOLSHEVIKS

John Morison (*editor*)
ETHNIC AND NATIONAL ISSUES IN RUSSIAN AND EAST EUROPEAN HISTORY

Judith Pallot (*editor*)
TRANSFORMING PEASANTS
Society, State and the Peasantry, 1861–1930

Karen L. Ryan and Barry P. Scherr (*editors*)
TWENTIETH-CENTURY RUSSIAN LITERATURE

Richard Sakwa (*editor*)
THE EXPERIENCE OF DEMOCRATIZATION IN EASTERN EUROPE

Ray Taras (*editor*)
NATIONAL IDENTITIES AND ETHNIC MINORITIES IN EASTERN EUROPE

Ian D. Thatcher (*editor*)
REGIME AND SOCIETY IN TWENTIETH-CENTURY RUSSIA

International Council for Central and East European Studies
Series Standing Order ISBN 0–333–71195–5
(*outside North America only*)

You can receive future titles in this series as they are published by placing a standing order. Please contact your bookseller or, in case of difficulty, write to us at the address below with your name and address, the title of the series and the ISBN quoted above.

Customer Services Department, Macmillan Distribution Ltd, Houndmills, Basingstoke, Hampshire RG21 6XS, England

Perspectives on Modern Central and East European Literature

Quests for Identity

Selected Papers from the Fifth World Congress of Central and East European Studies

Edited by

Todd Patrick Armstrong
Grinnell College
Iowa
USA

First published 2001 by
PALGRAVE
Houndmills, Basingstoke, Hampshire RG21 6XS and
175 Fifth Avenue, New York, N. Y. 10010
Companies and representatives throughout the world

PALGRAVE is the new global academic imprint of
St. Martin's Press LLC Scholarly and Reference Division and
Palgrave Publishers Ltd (formerly Macmillan Press Ltd).

ISBN 0–333–92161–5

This book is printed on paper suitable for recycling and made from fully managed and sustained forest sources.

A catalogue record for this book is available from the British Library.

Library of Congress Cataloging-in-Publication Data
World Congress for Central and East European Studies (5th : 1995 : Warsaw, Poland)
    Perspectives on modern Central and East European literature : quests for identity : selected papers from the Fifth World Congress of Central and East European Studies / edited by Todd Patrick Armstrong.
      p. cm.
    Includes bibliographical references and index.
    ISBN 0–333–92161–5
    1. East European literature—20th century—History and criticism—Congresses. I. Armstrong, Todd Patrick. II. Title.
    PN849.E9 W667 1995
    891.8—dc21
                              00–062595

10   9   8   7   6   5   4   3   2   1
10 09 08 07 06 05 04 03 02 01

Printed in Great Britain by Antony Rowe Ltd, Chippenham, Wiltshire

For Hanna, Alexander and Patrick

Contents

General Editor's Introduction

It is a great pleasure for me to introduce these volumes of papers that originated in the Fifth World Congress of Central and East European Studies, held in Warsaw in the week 6–11 August 1995, under the auspices of the International Council for Central and East European Studies and of the Institute of Philosophy and Sociology and the Institute of Political Studies of the Polish Academy of Sciences.

In the period since the previous World Congress, held in Harrogate, England, in July 1990, that part of the world that is the focus of Slavists' special attention had undergone the completion of changes that were already in train but the outcome of which was still uncertain. Moreover, given the inevitable time-lag between the conception of a major scholarly event and its occurrence, the major concerns at the beginning of the decade were not yet those of charting and analysing the transition from communist rule to some other form of political, economic and social entity and the impact of this on the societies and cultures of Russia, the Soviet Union and the countries loosely referred to as 'Eastern Europe': far less ambitious expectations were still the order of the day. Even though Poland had led the way in abandoning communist rule, shortly followed by all the other countries in 'Eastern Europe', it took some considerable imagination and conviction for the Executive Committee of the International Council to take the bold decision to hold the 1995 Congress in Eastern Europe, a decision that evoked a very positive response from our colleagues in Warsaw.

The different international climate immediately made itself felt, as scholars from the region were able to attend in large numbers a conference organised by a body that had been almost exclusively 'Western' in its previous experience. No longer were they specially invited guests (who on previous occasions had sometimes been denied exit visas to attend such Congresses), and it was a moving experience for me, as General Editor of the Congress proceedings, to receive letters and other communications by fax and e-mail from countries that in 1990 had no separate existence, or from provincial cities in the heart of post-Soviet Russia. Moreover, the opening of archives and the opportunities for new kinds of research, by scholars based in the countries concerned and by those entering from outside, meant that by 1995 there was much new information available, and scholars from the two 'sides' inevitably had much to say to one another.

The traditions in which the different groups had been trained meant that the styles of scholarship were not totally compatible, and there is a learning process in train that is likely to continue for some years. However, both the Congress itself and, more especially, the collaborative ventures such as this series of volumes containing selected papers, give opportunities for professional colleagues from around the world to make their own contributions to the new (and sometimes old) scholarly debates in ways that were hitherto impossible.

While not every paper that was presented or offered for publication was considered suitable for inclusion in the various thematic volumes, and individual editors sometimes had to make difficult choices and disappoint some authors, the endeavour as a whole must itself be seen as part of the global process of learning about the Slavic, Eurasian and Central and East European world: its peoples, its languages, its literature and cultural life, its history, politics, societies, economies, and its links with the rest of the world. Interest in the region is likely to grow, with new opportunities for contacts at various levels, and these volumes will, I am certain, serve both to educate and to inspire scholars and students anxious to understand.

It is very pleasant indeed to acknowledge once again the association of the Congress and the International Council with the publisher, and particularly the highly professional support and the keen personal interest of Tim Farmiloe for the whole project. If I may add a personal note, I should like to express my gratitude to John Morison and the Executive Committee of the International Council for charging me with the function of General Editor; to the editors of individual volumes, to whom fell the difficult tasks of assessment and selection followed by the tedium of editorial preparation; to my wife, Ethna, for her assistance in keeping track of several hundred typescripts, letters, faxes and e-mail messages; and to the many scholars who have patiently (and sometimes not so patiently – such are the pressures of modern academic life!) contributed to this complex international publishing venture. The collapse of communist rule has contributed sharply to globalisation, and the creation of this series of volumes has placed me at the hub of a world-wide enterprise, with editors on several continents and authors located in many countries of the world. It has provided me with a new kind of learning process for which I am humbly grateful.

Trinity College, Dublin RONALD J. HILL

Acknowledgements

Many people have contributed in many ways, great and small, to the completion of this collection. First and foremost, I would like to express my gratitude and appreciation to the authors and translators of the essays – for the insight I gained from their work, for the patience with which they endured the vagaries of the editing process, and for the readiness with which they responded to my many queries. I would like to thank my colleagues in the Russian Department at Grinnell College, John Mohan and Anatoly Vishevsky, for their support and encouragement in this endeavour, and to a number of Grinnell students who helped with matters of language, including Iva Frkić, Vadim Marchuk, Kara McCarty and Zorka Milin. Many thanks go to Terri Phipps, whose tireless efforts and assistance were invaluable. I also am grateful to Grinnell College for financial support – for funding both my attendance at the Warsaw Congress and my work on this book. To Professor Jerzy Krzyżanowski I am indebted for guidance in my work on Miłosz, which began in his graduate course on Polish literature. Konrad and Alicja Sadkowski and Michał and Judit Korpalski offered moral and intellectual support. Finally, I wish to express my gratitude to my family: to Hanna, who turned my gaze to Poland in the first place, and who stood by me with unflagging support throughout this arduous task, and to my sons Alexander Jan, our 'Polak mały', and Patrick Konrad, whose difficult beginning and miracle of survival, while somewhat slowing down my work on this book, inspired me to reach its end.

Grinnell College, Iowa   TODD PATRICK ARMSTRONG

Notes on the Contributors

Todd Patrick Armstrong is Assistant Professor of Russian at Grinnell College in Grinnell, Iowa. He has studied at the Universities of Warsaw and Wrocław, Poland, and at the University of Sofia, Bulgaria, and received his PhD in Russian with a secondary specialisation in Polish literature at The Ohio State University in 1993. His research and teaching interests, in addition to Russian language and literature, focus on the literature of Poland, with particular emphasis on the poetry and prose of Czesław Miłosz, and on broader issues in modern Central and Eastern European literature and culture. He has also contributed to a companion guide to the English translation of Henryk Sienkiewicz's *Ogniem i mieczem* (*With Fire and Sword*).

Lubica Babotová received her PhD in 1986 from the Faculty of Arts and Sciences at Presov University (formerly Safarik University) in Presov, Slovakia, where she currently teaches. She is author of *Transcarpathian Ukrainian Prose of the Second Half of the 19th Century* (1994) and has published over 150 articles dealing with Transcarpathian Ukrainian literature of the eighteenth, nineteenth and twentieth centuries in Canada, USA, Ukraine, Yugoslavia, Hungary, the Czech Republic and the Slovak Republic; she has also published a number of translations of Ukrainian literature into Czech and Slovak. She was Visiting Professor in the Department of Slavic Languages and Literatures at the University of Toronto in 1993–95, and is a member of the Advisory Board of the *Journal of Ukrainian Studies*.

George Gömöri is a native of Hungary. He has been living in England since 1956 and is Lecturer in Polish and Hungarian at the Univeristy of Cambridge. His publications include a book on modern Polish and Hungarian poetry (1966), several books on Norwid (*Cyprian Norwid,* 1974, and a collections of essays, co-edited with H. Mazur in 1989) and books of translations of Hungarian poets. His latest publication is an anthology of modern Hungarian poetry, *The Colonnade of Teeth* (co-edited with George Szirtes, 1996).

Diana A. Kuprel holds a PhD in Comparative Literature from the University of Toronto. She is currently a post-doctoral fellow on the Literary History Project at the University of Toronto.

Jelena Milojković-Djurić received her PhD from the University of Belgrade in 1981. She has taught at the University of Belgrade, the University of Colorado, and Texas A&M University. She is author of *Tradition and Avant-Garde: Literature and Arts in Serbian Culture* (East European Monographs, Vols 1 and 2, Boulder, CO, 1984 and 1988); *Aspects of Soviet Culture: Voices of Glasnost' 1960–1990* (East European Monographs, 1991); and *Panslavism and National Identity in Russia and in the Balkans 1830–1880: Images of the Self and Others* (East-European Monographs, 1994). She has published articles in a number of journals, including *Slavic Review, Studia Baltica Stockholmiensia, Serbian Academy of Sciences and Arts, East European Quarterly, Balcanica, Osteuropaforschung, Serbian Studies* and *Balkanistica.*

Larissa M. L. Z. Onyshkevych, since receiving her PhD from the University of Pennsylvania, has published extensively on Ukrainian and comparative drama. She is the editor and author of essays in *The Twins Shall Meet Again: An Anthology of Ukrainian Drama in Diaspora* (in Ukrainian, 1997) and *An Anthology of Modern Ukrainian Drama* (Vol. I, in Ukrainian, 1998; Vol. II, in English, forthcoming), and editor and co-translator of 'Ukrainian Poetry' (in Walter Cummins, ed., *Shifting Borders: Eastern European Poetries of the Eighties*, 1993). She has taught at Rutgers University, New Jersey, and is the past president of the Princeton Research Forum.

Dubravka Oraić-Tolić was born in Slavonski Brod, Republic of Croatia, in 1943, and she studied Philosophy and Russian Literature at the Faculty of Philosophy, University of Zagreb. She writes poems, essays and scholarly articles. She is currently a Professor of Literary Theory in the Department of Slavic Studies in the Faculty of Philosophy at the University of Zagreb. She is the author of *Urlik Amerike* (*The American Scream*, Zagreb, 1981); *Teorija citatnosti* (*Theory of Citation*, Zagreb, 1990), *Književnost i sudbina* (*Literature and Destiny*, Zagreb), and *Paradigme 20. stoljeća* (*Paradigms of the 20th Century*, Zagreb, 1996).

Marko Pavlyshyn is the head of Slavic Studies at Monash University in Melbourne and the president of the Australia and New Zealand Slavists' Association. He received his PhD from Monash University in 1983, and is the author of *Kanon ta ikonostas* (*Canon and Iconostasis*, Kyiv, 1997) and more than 50 articles and chapters on recent and contemporary Ukrainian literature. He is the editor of *Glasnost' in Context* (New York, 1990) and *Stus iak tekst* (*Stus as Text*, Melbourne, 1992); the translator into English of Yuri Andrukhovych's *Recreations* (Edmonton, 1998); and the co-editor of several scholarly collections. In 1995 Dr Pavlyshyn received the O. I. Biletsky Prize for literary and cultural criticism, conferred by the Writers' Union of Ukraine and the Ukrainian Ministry of Press and Information.

Halina Stephan is a Professor in the Department of Germanic and Slavic Studies at the University of Florida; she has also taught at the University of Southern California. She is the author of *LEF and the Left Front of the Arts* (1981), *Mrożek* (1996), and *Transcending the Absurd: Drama and Prose of Sławomir Mrożek* (1996). She has published articles on Russian avant-garde literature, Russian science fiction, women's literature, and Polish drama.

Małgorzata Sugiera is Professor at the Jagiellonian University in Cracow, Poland, and the head of the newly founded Drama Department at the Institute of Polish. She lectures on drama and theatre of the twentieth century, and the main field of her research is the theory and history of modern European and Polish drama. She is author of *Between Tradition and Avant-garde: The Theatre of Jerzy Grzegorzewski* (1993); *Sławomir Mrożek, the Playwright* (1995); and *Variations on Shakespeare in the Post-War European Drama* (1997). She has published over 100 articles in Poland and abroad, and translated over 25 articles on drama and theatre into Polish from English, German and French, including a translation of J. L. Styan's three volume study *Modern Drama in Theory and Practice* (Ossolineum, 1995). She was a Research Fellow of the Alexander von Humboldt Foundation during 1995–97, studying modern German language drama. Her latest book, *In the Shadow of Brecht: German Language Drama 1945–1995*, was published in the spring of 1999.

1 Introduction
Quests for Identity in Modern Central and East European Literature

Todd Patrick Armstrong

For the first time in its history, the World Congress on Central and East European Studies was held in a country – Poland – that belongs to the target area of study, an almost inconceivable notion in the field for many years, for obvious ideological reasons. Only with the fall of the Iron Curtain in the late 1980s and early 1990s did the opportunity for holding a congress in a newly independent capital present itself, and the Poles successfully lobbied for the honour. They also brought to the process the weighty baggage of 45 years of Soviet rule – a fact not without some consequence in the event. In early negotiations concerning the official languages of the conference, for example, the Polish organising committee apparently insisted on English as the language of the congress, and was less than eager to allow Russian as an official language. Of course, the desire to exclude or limit the language of the former Soviet oppressor is understandable, although not necessarily acceptable and hardly laudable in so far as many of the delegates to the congress were either from or specialised in Russia and the former Soviet states, and in so far as Russia itself can be counted as a part of Central and Eastern Europe. In another obvious, and somewhat dubious, gesture to the East, the organisers created an intriguing official emblem for the congress – the caricature of Stalin's infamous 'gift' to the Polish people, the monolithic Palace of Culture. The emblem is suggestive of what I consider a core theme of the Central and East European experience, the quest for identity, and a discussion of the building and its symbolism forms a fitting introduction to the present volume of proceedings on the literature of Central and Eastern Europe.

I first encountered this building in 1984, as I exited Warsaw's Central railway station; very much taken aback, I thought that I had perhaps taken the wrong train, and had returned to Moscow. Intrigued by the building, the architectural style of which we as exchange students in the volatile and interesting 1980s liked to call 'evil Gothic', I researched its origins. As was typical of the communist period, the glory of receiving this gift from Stalin and the Soviet workers was extolled, as was the appropriateness of the structure on Warsaw's skyline (there had even been a competition of designs!), while the obvious truth was officially ignored – namely, the ideological function of the structure as a reminder of Soviet domination.[1] In addition to the Academy of Sciences and a maze of administrative offices, the building housed one of the best Russian bookshops in Warsaw at the time, a frequent stop in the daily routine of a budding Slavist, and so I became quite well acquainted with some of its more interesting nooks and crannies: the statue of the worker, who held a stone tablet from which 'Stalin' (after 'Marx', 'Engels' and 'Lenin') had been visibly removed; the original name of the building – 'Pałac kultury i nauki imiena Jozefa Stalina' ('The Josef Stalin Palace of Culture and Science') obstructed to the casual observer by a neon sign which simply dropped the reference to Stalin.

Perhaps the most impressive – or oppressive? – thing about the place was its sprawling, labyrinthine quality. Indeed, this deliberately grandiose building, like its counterparts in other Warsaw Pact capitals (for example, the party buildings in Sofia, the Casa Scînteii in Bucharest, or the Hotel International in Prague) and the seven arche-typal structures in Moscow, was emblematic of the Soviet system – pervasive and invasive, enigmatic and confusing in its size and organisation. It is fitting that the hero in novelist Jerzy Kosiński's *Cockpit* creates a team of important academicians, entirely fictitious personae who are based in this Orwellian edifice, and through whose almost magical power he is able to engineer his escape from communist Poland to the West.

The building's depiction in the Congress emblem shows a stylised version of the building on a green and blue summer landscape, framed in bright yellow. The building itself is rent asunder with a jagged line, reminiscent of a bolt of lightning down the centre:

While heads would have rolled in the so-called good old days for such an obvious affront to the Eastern neighbour, to 'Big Brother', the new historical and political circumstances make such an obvious note of defiance not only possible, but perhaps inevitable as well. More importantly, the picture, emblazoned on the Congress programme and elsewhere, underlines the quest for identity in Central and East European culture and literature: in searching for one's own identity, one frequently begins by defining what one is not. It should come as no surprise that one way for the Poles to define themselves in the new political climate is by stating who they are not: 'We are no longer part of the Soviet (or Russian) Empire' – a sentiment surely not lost on participants from the new Russia or from the newly independent states so recently under the sway of Soviet influence. That this defiance is still problematic was confirmed to me when I inquired at the registration desk where I might obtain a copy of a poster with the emblem: I was told quite perfunctorily that they were not available, with a definite echo of the recent past, when such gestures of defiance were made, but not without considerable risk. And, of course, we should not forget that the physical structure of the former Palace of Culture still stands, serving still as a reminder of the past, housing not only the Academy of Sciences, but a business school and various commercial enterprises, and still hosting conferences, exhibitions and various cultural events; ironically, an early post-Soviet occupant was a casino. The building is also surrounded by a profusion of entrepreneurial energy which covers the 'tundra' (as plac Defilad, the site of many a May Day march, is ironically termed in Kosiński's novel). Finally, the more recent picture postcards of this former outpost of the empire, juxtaposed as they are to the warren of the thriving post-communist market-place or the monumental McDonald's restaurant across Marszałkowska Street, present, in a sense, images parallel to that found on the congress emblem – ambivalent symbols of ideological and cultural clashes in a radically changing, post-Soviet world.

In conversations with Czesław Miłosz, the poet Joseph Brodsky was wont to call the region in question 'Western Asia', in ironic reaction to the term 'Eastern Europe'.[2] In point of fact, it is no simple task to define an area in which borders have as a rule been fluid, where competing empires have divided the region over the centuries with little regard for its inhabitants or their desires. And in the twentieth century, the time-frame represented in the present volume, the domination of the Soviet Union in this sphere made most definitions politically sensitive, ideologically-bound. Which countries ought to be included in the notion of a 'Central and Eastern Europe'? Perhaps here we can rely on Milan Kundera, who saw this cultural space as comprising Poland, Hungary, the Czech Republic and Slovakia; the countries of the former Yugoslavia; the Baltic countries of Latvia, Lithuania and Estonia; Ukraine and Belarus; and the countries of the Balkans – Romania, Moldova and Bulgaria – countries which, as the Czech author has noted, were in the Soviet period 'threatened with the loss of their cultural and spiritual identity',[3] and which now are faced with new challenges in determining their 'cultural and spiritual' identities. For the most part, the essays that are included in this volume, while examining diverse literary, political and national experiences, nevertheless concern themselves in some sense with modern – that is, twentieth-century – issues of identity in Central and Eastern Europe. Efforts were made to include in the collection as many as possible of the national literatures discussed at the Congress, and the present volume contains essays on the literatures of Ukraine, Poland, Hungary, Croatia and Serbia.

The literature of Ukraine, a nation clearly undergoing an intense struggle to find its place in the post-Soviet era, finds voice in three of the essays in this volume. Marko Pavlyshyn focuses on the positioning of recent Ukrainian literature in a post-colonial context (in the sense that Ukraine was colonised by the Russian, that is Soviet, Empire). Adopting and adapting the terminology of colonial studies, Pavlyshyn presents a coherent survey of recent and current trends in contemporary Ukrainian literature, where issues of 'cultural and spiritual identity' feature prominently. Focusing on generational divisions in the post-colonial context, Pavlyshyn examines groups of writers who 'seek to affirm and develop essentially traditional views of the function of literature in society,' and also those who 'seek to challenge and subvert' these views, creating in the process consciously transgressive works that turn a sceptical eye towards 'received cultural inheritances' – vestiges of 'official Soviet culture' and a liberating national Ukrainian literature. Interrogating a national identity, many young writers resist the creation of a 'Ukraino-centric' mythology, opting instead for an examination of the complex amalgam of Russian and Ukrainian cultures, the nature and function of literature, and the 'interpenetration of colonial and anti-colonial'. Pavlyshyn suggests that the youngest writers are engaging in nascent post-colonial frameworks, writing, as he notes, 'without the millstone of duty to an imperative of liberation around its neck' (a defining feature, it can be argued, of much of the literature of Central and Eastern Europe until the break-up of the Soviet Union).

A rather different issue concerns Larissa M. L. Z. Onyshkevych, who, in her essay on censorship, draws on the literature of twentieth-century Ukrainian authors writing under the conditions of Soviet (and, briefly, Nazi) censorship. Onyshkevych probes the thorny issue of determining a definitive literary text when dealing with multiple variants created under the watchful eye of the (primarily political) censor. Using as an exemplary case Mykola Kulish's *Sonata Pathétique* – whose odyssey of publication and performance in many ways charts the vagaries of Ukrainian fate during this century – she shows how the multiple versions suggest the need for a new approach by the literary scholar. Her essay moves towards an understanding of the intrusion of history and society into the fate of a literary work, and reveals the complex and problematic interrelationship between author, censor and text.

Transcarpathian Rus' – a geographical area falling across the borders of a number of nations and struggling throughout its history to define its cultural and political identity – forms the focus of Lubica Babotová's essay on twentieth-century Transcarpathian Ukrainian literature. She analyses the historical development of the literary process in the region, examining the major periods of the twentieth century. Babotová emphasises not only the many factors that combined to influence the writers of succeeding generations, but, using publication histories, she discusses the very emergence of a Transcarpathian literature. The quest for identity and national awareness in this literature finds expression in, among other things, questions of language: the inter-war period, for example, found a kind of literary diglossia, with some writers opting for Ukrainian, and promoting a return to the people, and others writing in Russian, and advocating union with Russia – issues relevant in the post-Soviet context as well.

Central and Eastern European literature, as mentioned in the opening remarks, remains bound by the shackles of a tragic history, with cultural and national identity and political autonomy ever in question – a notion reflected in several of the essays in this collection. For example, the struggle of art against totalitarianism concerns the art of Polish poets of the New Wave and the Hungarian poet György Petri, as examined by George Gömöri. He finds several parallels in the poetic formulations of Polish and Hungarian literary responses to the turbulent events of 1968–70, focusing primarily on the importance of language for poets struggling to find expression in the waning decades of communism. In the Polish context, such poets as Barańczak, Krynicki and Zagajewski, as the author points out, in developing their poetic theories were fighting against the manipulation and subjugation of language by the regime. As Gömöri suggests, the Polish New Wave's characteristic openness, its 'farewell to the wonderland of illusions', anticipated the spirit of Solidarity – arguably a major component of an evolving Polish identity that arose in the 1980s and 1990s.

In the Hungarian context, a single poet is considered, György Petri, in whose work can be found a similar concern with language, although Petri is shown to take the path of a 'brutal outspokenness', aiming to shock the political establishment. While never delving into abstract poetic theory, Petri none the less comes to similar conclusions regarding language: 'what was important from the beginning is that you have to name things properly'. A similar judgement is found in the prose of Czesław Miłosz, as analysed in Todd Patrick Armstrong's essay. He examines what he calls the 'quintessentially Polish theme' of the dilemma in *Seizure of Power*, a novel by the Polish Nobel Laureate, written in part as a response to Andrzejewski's *Ashes and Diamonds* and intended to convey the true complexities of the troubled period immediately following the war. Armstrong presents a structural analysis of the work, finding in Miłosz's use of a structural element – the frame – a key to understanding his thematics. Miłosz's own non-fictional and autobiographical treatises on issues involving Central European identity are brought to bear in his argument, and are shown to inform the poetics of his novel. Throughout his essay, Armstrong underlines the ambiguities of choice – a pertinent and ever-problematic issue in the current transition from communist to democratic rule: witness, for example, the numerous legal and ethical quagmires encountered in the search for guilt and complicity after years of political repression under totalitarian regimes.

The writer in exile and emigration has traditionally been a major force in the literature of this region (indeed, the predominant themes of the Central European Literature proceedings of the IV ICCEES Congress in Harrogate concerned writing in exile). Three expatriate Polish writers are examined in the essays in this volume: Sławomir Mrożek, Janusz Głowacki, and Witold Gombrowicz. Analysing the plays of the first two Polish émigré playwrights mentioned, Halina Stephan sheds light on the problematic issues of identity involved in writing in emigration. Stephan examines the two writers' contrasting approaches to nationality and its role in their aesthetics. On one hand, as she demonstrates, Mrożek chooses to overcome his national culture as a marker and dominant feature of his art, attempting to move beyond the particular of the national experience, striving instead for the 'universal' in his plays. Janusz Głowacki, on the other hand, finds a way to accommodate his Polish heritage in the context of American culture. According to Stephan, he capitalises on his status as expatriate writer, and his plays are 'clearly rooted to the concept of nationality'.

Małgorzata Sugiera offers a close study of Sławomir Mrożek's dramatic art in her analysis of three of his plays, *On Foot*, *Portrait*, and *Love in the Crimea*. Her primary concern is Mrożek's vision of twentieth-century history and the various ways in which it is explored in these three works. *On Foot*, according to Sugiera, is not only a 'camouflaged autobiographical play', an examination of the post-war generation, but a presentation of a 'philosophy of history' as well. *Portrait*, which unfolds in the Stalin era, in this context represents a search for the 'truth of the world' in historicity, the 'unpredictability of life', and 'chaos'. The Chekhovian *Love in the Crimea* is seen as a 'pamphlet in dramatic form', a testament to Mrożek's fascination with and ultimate struggle 'to flee from History'. Diana A. Kuprel in her study of Gombrowicz investigates his philosophical approach to intersubjectivity, or, as he termed it, 'interhumanity' – and the notion of form so important in the Polish writer's aesthetic and *Weltanschauung*. Less concerned than other writers analysed in this collection with more localised issues of national, social, historical or political identity, Gombrowicz, as Kuprel shows, instead engages in a decidedly modern ontological analysis and interrogation of traditional views of the universal human condition. Kuprel presents three manifestations of how his 'interhumanity' functions in and informs his dramatic works – the hermeneutic, the dialogic and the semiotic, uncovering in the process the complex multivalent layerings of interrelationships between self and other, form and formlessness, and the substance of human identity as a product of these interrelationships.

Serbian women writers in emigration are the focus of Jelena Milojković-Djurić's study, in which she examines the poetics of exile. Intended as an introduction to the work of poets who emigrated as a result of the Second World War and its aftermath (Kosara Gavrilović and Milena Miličić) or for other extenuating circumstances (Milica Miladinović and Ljiljana Vukić), an important aspect of her essay concerns the poets' biographies and their respective publication histories. Milojković-Djurić shows how exile and the hardships of 'cultural alterity' not only affected these women writers' lives, but also found expression in their poetry, a number of examples of which are presented and analysed in her work. The themes and images of separation and anguish, of isolation and memory, are familiar characteristics of exile literature, and so it comes as no surprise that they comprise dominant features of these poets' works. Another, no less important, aspect of their poetry is found in the varied approaches to subject matter that are at the same time united in their feminine themes and perspective; for example, Vukić's poem 'Majke' ('Mothers') is a testimony to mothers everywhere, paying tribute to the nurturing power of motherhood.

The tragedy of the 1990s in the former Yugoslavia lay bare in an extremely concentrated and violent form many of the unresolved issues of identity – ethnic, religious, cultural, political – that have plagued the entire region of Central and Eastern Europe for most of its modern history. The final work included in this collection, by the Croatian poet and literary theorist Dubravka Oraić-Tolić, takes the form of an epistolary essay that is at once both a profound theoretical piece and an impassioned plea for a solution to the grim tragedy that has consumed the Balkans in recent years. It is another kind of quest on the part of its author: a quest for her identity as poet, a search for the meaning of her 1981 poem *Urlik Amerike* ('*American Scream*'), the meaning of which in the context of war-torn 1990s Croatia is transformed, and demands a new reading. Her 'letter' – addressed to the American ambassador – is a forum in which she struggles to find the evolving identity of her text, first in the 1970s and 1980s, and finally 'on the eve of the end of the twentieth century' – precisely when her poem acquired a new urgency and importance. Oraić-Tolić presents a sophisticated and intriguing analysis of the Modern era in European civilisation, an analysis which informs her understanding of the 'first post-modern war on the soil of Europe' – a reference, of course, to the war in the former Yugoslavia. Her poignant letter is also an appeal to the West – to America, as an inheritor of modern European history – to respond to the horror in the former Yugoslavia, to rescue what she defines as a new concept of freedom: the 'simple and intimate freedom of space'. She has in mind one of the most fundamental aspects of human identity: our right to an address, a home, a physical space – a part of the Balkan identity that has certainly been called into question in the 1990s. Her essay is especially relevant in a collection of works about the literature of Central and Eastern Europe, a region where issues of freedom, of space, and of identity have been and remain in the forefront.

Notes

1 For an illuminating discussion of these and other ideologically-oriented structures in Eastern Europe, see Åman Anders, *Architecture and Ideology in Eastern Europe during the Stalin Era: An Aspect of Cold War History* (The Architectural History Foundation, Inc., New York) (Cambridge, MA: MIT Press, 1992).

2 Czesław Miłosz, 'Central European Attitudes', Cross Currents 5: A Yearbook of Central European Culture (1986), pp. 101–8.

3 Roman Szporluk quotes Kundera in his essay, 'Defining "Central Europe": Power, Politics, and Culture', *Cross Currents 1: A Yearbook of Central European Culture* (1982), pp. 1–11.

2 Demystifying High Culture?

'Young' Ukrainian Poetry and Prose in the 1990s

Marko Pavlyshyn

In its attempts to categorise and describe literary developments in Ukraine in recent decades, literary scholarship and criticism in Ukraine and in the West has found much utility in the notion of the generation or, more precisely, the age cohort. This is not surprising. In a controlled cultural system, where the individual literary work is expected to respond to precise definitions of its ideological function and where the activity of the writer is strongly influenced by direct official pressures, one might expect fluctuations in the political climate to impinge directly upon the literary sphere. In particular, one might expect writers at the beginning of their careers to react in broadly similar ways to the configuration of culture and politics prevailing at the time of their formation as writers.

Thus, the term 'shistdesiatnyky' – 'people of the sixties' – serves quite well as a group designation for the most prominent of the critics, poets and prose writers who, born in the 1930s, responded to the brief cultural liberalisation of the early 1960s. 'Visimdesiatnyky' ('people of the eighties'), a term whose circulation has been reinforced by the publication in 1990 of a well-edited anthology of the same name,[1] refers to the poets and writers, many, though not all, born in the late 1950s and early 1960s, who came into public view before and during the years of *glasnost'*. The *visimdesiatnyky* share a literary education probably more sophisticated and specialised than that of any preceding generation. They are united, for all their considerable thematic and stylistic differences, by complexity, self-consciousness, and awareness of the literary traditions within which they stand. An important minority among them, comprising the Bu-Ba-Bu group and others, undertook in the early 1990s the bold project of questioning and destabilising those traditions.

It was, no doubt, partly because of such gestures of rebellion, which peaked more or less at the time of the collapse of the USSR and the declaration of independence by Ukraine, that the literary works of this cohort were frequently referred to as representing 'young' Ukrainian poetry and prose. Since 1993 this appellation has been challenged by an even younger group: poets and writers born at the end of the 1960s and in the early 1970s. These new literati, apparently not perturbed by the collapse of the elite status of the writing profession in the wake of the marketisation of culture, nor discouraged by the radical shrinkage of opportunities for publication, have formed a loose grouping called Creative Association 500. They have also won the benevolent attention and patronage of Osyp Zinkevych, whose publishing house, Smoloskyp, in 1994 brought out their anthology *Molode vyno* (*Young wine*). The title, alluding to the Gospel admonition not to pour new wine into old skins, suggests – perhaps misleadingly, as we shall see – that the content of the anthology is incompatible with the available containers of previous literary practices.

It is this relationship of recent Ukrainian writing, both young and youngest, to old cultural 'skins' that I wish to examine in this chapter. Some representatives of the new writing seek to affirm and develop essentially traditional views of the function of literature in society. Others seek to challenge and subvert them. I wish to consider these various positions in the context of changes in the disposition of cultural power and authority since the fall of the USSR, and to test the extent to which they may be regarded as 'post-colonial'.

The term 'post-colonial' I use here in the specific and limited sense which I have sought to define in some detail elsewhere.[2] As a chronological term (meaning 'pertaining to the period after the international recognition of a former colony as independent'), 'post-colonial' has little critical utility. It acquires analytic force if juxtaposed to the concepts of the 'colonial' and the 'anti-colonial.' It is useful to regard as 'colonial' those cultural phenomena which may be interpreted as promoting or maintaining the structures and myths of colonial power relations, and as 'anti-colonial' those which directly challenge or seek to invert such relations. The attribute 'post-colonial' applies to those entities in culture which recognise the real and implicit violence of the colonial, on the one hand, and the reactive and limited quality of the anti-colonial, on the other. The post-colonial is that which, conscious of the simultaneous availability of the heritage of the colonial and the anti-colonial, identifies with neither; yet, in its efforts to go beyond the structures of domination left behind from the colonial age, it can (and, indeed, often cannot but) invoke both.

There is no doubt that the term 'post-colonial,' used in this way, acquires an evaluative dimension. Within a system of political judgements that ascribes high value to eliminating the consequences of colonial domination, the post-colonial naturally ranks more highly than the colonial. It also ranks more highly than the anti-colonial, which preserves the structures of the colonial by directly negating them. This needs to be stated, lest it appear that, by describing a phenomenon as 'post-colonial', we merely impartially categorise it. In fact, to argue that a product of culture is 'post-colonial' is to align it with a process that, in an explicitly partisan way, we consider desirable, believing that it increases human freedom and diminishes the oppressive exercise of power.

How post-colonial, then, are the various nuances of the 'young' and the 'youngest' Ukrainian poetry and prose? It seems logical to begin with a consideration of those events in Ukrainian literature which, in the years immediately preceding and immediately following the Ukrainian declaration of independence in December 1991, attracted the most public attention: the literary provocations and scandals. Grandest among them was the staging in the L'viv opera house over four nights in Autumn 1992 of the carnivalesque extravaganza 'Chrysler Imperial', a joint project of the three poets united in the Bu-Ba-Bu group – Iurii Andrukhovych, Oleksandr Irvanets' and Viktor Neborak.

The activity of Bu-Ba-Bu – their publications and happenings – was merely the most elaborate and visible manifestation of a much wider phenomenon. Other young poets, no less interested in breaking taboos, experimenting with form, and alternating between esotericism and obscenity, organised themselves into no less provocatively or mysteriously named collectives (most of them, like Bu-Ba-Bu, comprising three members, all males): Luhosad (Meadow Orchard: Ivan Luchuk, Nazar Honchar and Roman Sadlovs'kyi), Propala hramota (Lost Document: Semen Lybon', Iurko Pozaiak and Viktor Nedostup, pseudonyms of Oleksii Semenchenko, Iurii Lysenko and Viktor

Lapkin, respectively), and the slightly later Nova deheneratsiia (New Degeneration: Ivan Andrusiak, Stepan Protsiuk and Ivan Tsyperdiuk). Some of their works appeared on the pages of the established literary journals.[3] A few new periodicals of unprecedented licentiousness sprang up – *Avzhezh* (*Of Course!*) in Zhytomyr, and the remarkable *Chetver* (*Thursday*) in Ivano-Frankivs'k. They were matched in provocativeness by the culture pages of the L'viv newspaper *PostPostup* (*PostProgress*) under the editorship of Iurii Vynnychuk.

In its strident challenges to aesthetic convention, in its self-irony, and in many individual echoes and allusions, the movement is reminiscent of the more radical artistic trends of the 1920s, and is frequently referred to in Ukraine for that reason – disparagingly, more often than not – as 'neo-avantgardism.[4] It is equally evident that, through its playfully intertextual attitude to tradition, its ironic refusal of philosophical certainties and its orientation on the pleasure-giving dimension of the work of art, the movement bears witness to its participation in global post-modernism. But even without being prompted by these labels – 'avantgardist' and 'postmodern' – we could scarcely fail to observe the extremely sceptical attitude of such young writing towards two received cultural inheritances: on the one hand, official Soviet culture (discredited by the turn of political events, it is perceived by them as a habit of thought, judgment and aesthetic production that is by no means defunct), and, on the other, the Great Tradition of Ukrainian literature as a weapon in the struggle for national liberation.

The scandalous quality of the Bubabists and other 'neo-avantgardists' is the consequence, in part, of deliberately transgressive gestures. Breaches of sexual decorum[5] – the depiction of sexual activity and, perhaps even less tolerable, the use of obscenity in literary texts, most notoriously in Andrukhovych's short novel *Rekreatsii* (*Recreations*, 1992) – in at least some instances attracted the outrage which they appeared designed to elicit. Thus, Iurii Mushketyk, head of the Writers' Union of Ukraine, defending 'eternal realism' against the encroachments and subversions of non-traditional writers, gives special attention to their 'licentiousness': 'disregard for traditional folk morality and ancient Ukrainian traditions has the consequence that the pages of novels, stories and long and short poems are full of ugly obscenities. [...] Obscenity demeans the artist, it places him on one level with the 'tomato-nosed slobs' that haunt the filthiest taverns, with the racketeers and agents of low-grade business.'[6] No less sanctimoniously condemned was the Bubabists' mocking attitude towards some of the icons of the Ukrainian literary tradition – most notably, Oleksandr Irvanets's poem 'Liubit'!' ('Love!,' 1992), which parodies Volodymyr Sosiura's patriotic poem 'Liubit' Ukrainu' ('Love Ukraine,' 1944):

> Любіть Оклахому! Вночі і в обід,
> Як неньку і дедді достоту.
> Любіть Індіану. Й так само любіть
> Північну й Південну Дакоту.[7]

> (Love Oklahoma! At night and at noon,
> As you love your mummy and daddy.
> Love Indiana. And don't love any less
> North and South Dakota).

Perhaps less stridently offensive to sensibilities accustomed to the demureness of official Soviet literature and its respect for prevailing cultural authority, but none the less transgressive and scandalous, were gestures of rejection of conventional literary form, indeed, of the platitudinous and prosaic diction of mainstream Soviet literature. In many cases this formal and stylistic dissent was innovative only in relation to its immediate context. Irrespective of whether this is coincidental or, as seems much more likely, deliberate, the linguistic games of Neborak, Irvanets', Nedostup or Pozaiak resonate with the experiments of the 1910s and 1920s. We encounter in Neborak, for example, the decay of the word as conventional signifier into sounds (or letters) that do not carry an agreed meaning:

> і в небес Ренесансу гряде
> МАСКА – ЛІТАЮЧА ГОЛОВА
> Я ЛІТАЮЧА ГОЛОВА
> ЯГОЛО ВАЛІ ТАЮЧА
> ЯГО ЛОВАЛІТА
> ЮЧА ГОЛО ВАЯ
> ЧАГОЛО...Ю...АЯ...АО...А...О... [8]

> (and into the Renaissance firmament advances
> THE MASK – A FLYING HEAD

I AM A FLYING HEAD
IAMAFLY INGHE AD
IA MAFLY/ ING HE ADI
NGHEA...I...YI...AE...A...E)

Prototypes of such verse abound in the European avant-garde and, closer to home, in the futurist poetry of Mykhail' Semenko. Perhaps there is an intended, and post-modern, irony in the fact that the demonstration of the contingent quality of the relationship between language and meaning can be performed in 1990 only as a quotation; that Neborak's avantgardism is, from a culturally informed perspective, an exercise not in innovation but in historicism. An even longer view would place both Neborak and Semenko in a tradition of subversions of the conventional function of the phoneme and the grapheme that stretches back to the baroque acrostic of Ioan Velychkovs'kyi. The formal gestures of the avantgardists, it might be argued, signal not merely a present and local challenge to the hegemony of common sense and plain speech, but allude (even within Ukrainian literature) to a whole tradition of such challenges – an alternative universe not dreamt of in the philosophy of Iurii Mushketyk.

Another dimension of much contemporary writing that renders it discreetly scandalous is its obscurity, a feature frequently connected to its emphasis on form. While not an affront to public taste, obscurity is an affront to common sense, as Pavlo Zahrebel'nyi's disarmingly forthright complaint at a young writers' seminar eloquently testifies: 'It has become extremely modish ... to write in an incomprehensible language that dispenses with words and punctuation marks. Quite often the authors of such writings themselves have no idea what they have written. We know from history that obscure language was used by slaves and criminals. Shevchenko, Pushkin, Tolstoy and Cervantes were transparent.'[9] Obscurity is, in high modernism, a feature of works which lay claim to privileged insight and profound meaning. It is also a powerful device for excluding the uninitiated and thus generating an esoteric elite of cognoscenti. But the same obscure work may support a reading both as a 'serious' text and as a *parody* upon a serious text. In the case of philosophical, or perhaps pseudo-philosophical, works such as Volodymyr Tsybul'ko's poem 'Muzei' ('Museum', 1992) it is impossible to tell. A pervasive motif of the poem is the thread of saliva, 'endless, like time itself',[10] that depends from a dog's mouth. The culturally alert reader is torn between the temptation to interpret this dark image symbolically, on the one hand, and to read it as a joke at the expense of overzealous exegetes, on the other. Obscurity is often intensified by reference to arcane authorities and unfamiliar or foreign contexts. Such effects are not infrequently sought by Tsybul'ko:

музей вивернутий як рукавичка
дім цей кам'яна епістола епохи барокко
епосі постмодернізму

обличчя директора печальне як псальма
   в молодості йому хотилося блукати
   зайнятися суфізмом
   і перекласти Джалалетдіна Румі[11]

(the museum is turned inside out like a glove
this building is a stone epistle of the age of the Baroque
to the epoch of postmodernism

the face of the director is sad as a psalm
   in his youth he wished to go wandering
   to study Sufism
   and to translate Jalal-ud-din Rumi)

These lines include the poetic persona in the set, doubtless rather select, of Ukrainian speakers who are at home both with recently-imported terminology of Western cultural studies, Sufism, and Persian poetry. They also exclude (and, by excluding, offend) the uninitiated.

On the other hand, it is clear that the public is capable of being as scandalised – offended by the breaching of its expectations – by literary texts that set their sights too low as by those that set them too high. Andrukhovych, Mikhalko Skalitski, Bohdan Zholdak, and Iurii Vynnychuk have in various ways sought to conflate high and popular art, to utilise some of the forms of audience appeal familiar to contemporary international mass culture, to imagine the reader not as a pupil but as a consumer – in a word, to make literature that gives pleasure. This is the case, for example, in Mikhalko Skalitski's short novel *Amin'* (*Amen*, 1993),[12] in which a homeless vagrant repeatedly – in his dreams – achieves the comfort of love and the liberation of death.

Skalitski combines the gentle and humane ethos which is the hallmark of his novel, and its artful fluctuations between realistic and fantastic discourses, with a well-constructed, interest-evoking plot and a leavening of scenes that are both sexually titillating and well written. The choir of scandalised responses to Andrukhovych's *Recreations* suggests that there were a good many readers who overcame their outrage to read the work to the end. The notion of the aesthetic text as a source of pleasure and as an object to be consumed is made especially palpable in the third issue of *Chetver* (1992), which is structured like an encyclopedia. Its alphabetically-ordered entries include whimsical biographies of the Bubabists and their friends, notes on theological, demonological, philosophical and cabbalistic topics, poems and short stories, and such seemingly random items as 'Russia', 'Phallus', 'Newton's apple' and 'Echidna'. The issue is breathtakingly illustrated with black-and-white computer graphics, montages and photographs, alongside old technical and zoological drawings, all splendidly unrelated to the text. What appears to be argued through this compositional principle of ordered randomness is the presence and attractiveness of all things in the alphabet – and, above all, their availability for easy location and rapid ingestion.

Not unexpectedly, such almost physiologically definable objectives for literature scandalise those who see the mission of literature as mimetic, utopian, transformative or missionary. Concerning this there is a remarkable consensus between a conservative such as Mushketyk, who demands of literature the 'true representation of reality',[13] and much younger writers who also conceptualise the purpose of literature in terms of elevated duties and obligations – Viacheslav Medvid', for example, for whom 'prose, like poetry, is a certain condition of the spirit, of being, in which the artist creates a new, artistic world according to divine laws,'[14] or Ievhen Pashkovs'kyi, who believes that 'literature renews that pure, childlike and merciful condition in which we were all innocent before God'.[15]

As far as its opponents are concerned, the literature of the scandalmakers is merely negative, indeed, destructive. It execrates, in the view of some, the tried and true values that stood the test even of Socialist Realism. In the view of others it despises the elevated and dignified vocation that literature after Socialist Realism is called upon to follow.

There is some truth in these opinions. In an obvious and superficial

but sometimes also ambiguous and incomplete way, these writings
implicitly – and some of their makers explicitly – oppose the literary
establishment and its chief edifice, the Writers' Union of Ukraine.
Their anarchic, subversive and carnivalesque quality is antithetical to
the very idea of an organised and hierarchical collective. On the other
hand, some of the more irate attacks upon the Union – that of Ihor
Malen'kyi, for example – have reflected not a desire to do away with it,
but to establish oneself within it in a suitably advantageous way.[16]

More substantive – although also not absolute – is the opposition
of this literary formation to the literature of dutiful anti-colonialism.
It refuses, in Andrukhovych's *Recreations* in particular, to celebrate
Literature and the Poet as vehicles for national liberation or consoli-
dation. It refuses to be complicit in a situation where, as Iaroslav
Mel'nyk has put it, 'we have made idols (ideals, temples, if you prefer)
of all of Ukraine's culturally significant figures; we pray to them; they
are taboo and the inquisitive and analytic mind may not approach
them'.[17] It refuses to participate in projects to replace Russo-centric
Soviet and pre-Soviet historical myths with Ukraino-centric ones. Thus,
Bohdan Zholdak's monologue 'Ne treba sliz' ('There is No Need for
Tears', 1994) is a satire on the delusions and obsessions of patriotic
amateur historians. It is no accident that the work is part of a cycle
entitled 'Colonial Apocrypha': Zholdak sees the temptation to distort
history in a way that glorifies one's own country as a mere reflection of
the opposite colonial tendency to marginalise and belittle it.

No less emphatic is the refusal to make a fetish of the central symbol
of anti-colonial identity, the national language. Zholdak, who writes
many of his stories in 'surzhyk', the non-standard mixture of Ukrainian
and Russian that is the real vernacular of many residents of Ukraine,
thereby signifies his location at the border – the contamination point –
between colonial and anti-colonial culture. On the one hand, surzhyk is
the outcome of the violence of the authoritative colonial culture against
the colonised indigenous idiom. By using surzhyk in literature, Zholdak
draws attention to, and thereby protests against, this fact. On the other
hand, surzhyk, mimetic as it is of majority language practice, also
points out the abstractness of the notion of the normative literary
language as a unifying experience in the life of the newly-independent
nation. Zholdak's texts render visible the irreversible interpenetration
of colonial and anti-colonial history. They refuse to lament this fact,

however. Through their vibrancy and humour they celebrate it as a liberating and fruitful point of departure for a post-colonial future.

It is this constructive and, in the final analysis, optimistic dimension that differentiates the literary scandalists of the 1990s from certain of their predecessors in the European avant-garde, whose destruction of language and of art partnered a profound scepticism concerning language and the aesthetic in general. Andrukhovych connects the activity of Bu-Ba-Bu to the rejuvenatory role of carnival laughter as imagined by Bakhtin: 'Carnival ... juggles hierarchical values, it turns the world upon its head, it provokes the most sacred ideas in order to rescue them from ossification and death.'[18] He also sees it as contributing to the maturation of Ukrainian literature by 'melting this iceberg of lenten under-educated seriousness that weighs upon everything Ukrainian'.[19]

In this conceptualisation of the ultimately civilising, normalising ('educating'!) role of transgressive writing there is, of course, an irreducible echo of the colonial inferiority complex that requires constant measurement of the ex-colonial self against outside standards – an echo that is more audible, perhaps, in Mykola Sulyma's pleasure in the fact that the activity of Propala hramota, even if belatedly, fills a certain cultural niche that Holoborod'ko and others had been prevented from filling in the late 1960s and early 1970s.[20] Andrukhovych and his colleagues, of course, are aware that the project of de-provincialising Ukrainian culture, by taking its bearings upon Western cultures or the culture of global post-modernism, runs the danger of merely exchanging colonial masters. The demonic Popel, the émigré who in *Recreations* returns from Switzerland with the hard currency that effortlessly purchases the labour and respect of young Ukrainian poets, is emblematic of such risks. But the project of post-colonialism, whose very purpose is to transcend the disempowering structures erected by colonialism, is imaginable only in terms of winning direct access to the global. The autarchic vision of self-contained and self-sufficient authenticity which is in Mushketyk's mind when he denounces any quest for innovation 'on foreign garbage dumps'[21] is a formula for perpetuating imposed colonial invisibility and disadvantage.

The adversaries opposed by the new transgressive writing, it should not be forgotten, include colonialism itself. Among the most telling depictions and critiques of colonialism as a present reality that is

complex, insidious and all-pervasive are Andrukhovych's novels
Recreations and *Moskoviiada* (*The Moscoviad*, 1993) – a fact that
has passed largely unnoticed in the debate surrounding them.[22]
Moskoviiada presents Moscow in grotesque refraction as the location
where the national and regional variety of the Soviet-Union-as-Empire
is constantly in evidence, but where each of the composite parts of the
whole is present only in degraded and corrupt form. Skalitski's *Amin'*
presents a rather similar image of the surzhyk-speaking society of
empire, but with the important proviso that the vileness of the system is
at every step subverted by individual human kindness.

To sum up the argument so far: the transgressive writing that is
sometimes regarded as merely scandalous is, precisely in its scandalous
quality, post-colonial. If we were to abstract from it a generalised
argument, we would say that it furnishes a sharp and, at times,
elaborate critique of the colonial while resisting the shallow ideologism
of the anti-colonial, whose tendency is merely to change the direction
of the distortions and repressions of the colonial without alleviating
them.

Among the writers of the same age cohort as the Bubabists there are
those who, like Ievhen Pashkovs'kyi and Viacheslav Medvid', explicitly conceive of themselves as standing in an adversarial relationship
with their carnivalist colleagues. Theirs is the prose that continues to
narrate the mainstream narrative of Ukrainian literature since the
nineteenth century: the story of larger or smaller tragedies of human
suffering that should move readers either to political action or to
generalised reflection upon the essentially unpleasant nature of reality.

Such works aspire to aesthetic distinction through their style. The
prose of Pashkovs'kyi, Medvid' or of Oles' Ulianenko, the author
of *Stalinka* (1994), a nightmarish narrative of the low-life and crimi-
nal underground in Kiev, intends to be art prose *par excellence*. It
possesses in high order that quality of obscurity and exclusiveness
whose function is to signal that the culture being created here is elitist.
Pashkovs'kyi cultivates the heroically long sentence (he reads like
Emma Andiievs'ka minus her grammatical subordination and wit).
Ulianenko specialises in the rare and remarkable word. This is literature
imagined as the noble burden of the artist, as the wrought product of
superhuman concentration and labour. It brings to mind the seriousness
and tragedy of Stefanyk.

This is, of course, a literature of opposition – not only in the partisan sense that it opposes the (historical, social, metaphysical) sources of human (especially Ukrainian) suffering, but also in the sense of offering a high art alternative to the graphomaniacal blandness of most Soviet prose. Its agenda – not only implicit, but explicitly enunciated, for example, on the pages of the journal *Osnova* – is to generate an elitist, authentic, home-grown culture capable once again, as Medvid' puts it, of 'giving voice to its essence through the grandiose music of the Ukrainian world-experience'.[23] Such writing, and such a theory of writing, are the very model of contemporary anti-colonialism. They continue the tradition of literature as the mirror of the nation and the repository of supreme national values. They assert the self of the nation by delimiting it against the nation's non-self. Medvid', in affirming such a dichotomy, invents the term 'kulturaboryhen' – cultural aborigine – to designate the ideal, uncontaminated, abstractly authentic local person. Perhaps the historical association of aboriginality, a term used most frequently with reference to the indigenous peoples of the white settler colonies, with disempowerment, colonial exploitation and, ultimately, loss of identity, has passed Medvid' by, as has the fact that a call for the cultural autarchy of an ex-colony is a call for its absence from global culture – an ideal pursued no less energetically, although for other reasons, by the colonial masters of the past.

The advocates of high national culture, serious and severe, then, are not post-colonial. What of the newcomers to the literary scene, members of the Creative Association 500? As far as can be judged from their published works and their self-commentaries, they are neither especially homogeneous, nor, as a group, especially affected by the tensions that polarise other parts of the literary world. They recognise their common professional interests, however, one of which is to market themselves as an absolute novelty under a common label and to differentiate themselves sharply from their predecessors, who, they suggest, have now been superseded. Thus, Maksym Rozumnyi, in his response to Mushketyk's 'Koleso', distances the members of his association from the 35-year-old Bubabists and other objects of Mushketyk's ire, referring to them as 'balding uncles.'[24] The manoeuvre is purely tactical, and does not reflect any rejection in principle of the credo of Bu-Ba-Bu. Indeed, Bu-Ba-Bu and Propala hramota enjoy the status of classics with some of them: Serhii Rudenko and Ivan Tsyperdiuk have written imitations, parodies and variations upon their work.

But, on the whole, Creative Association 500 has a relationship to literary tradition that is curiously unproblematic for a group in which there are so many trained philologists (twelve of the twenty poets represented in *Molode Vyno*). They unselfconsciously reinvent every available wheel. Most of them are involved – in general, in a very accomplished way – in the reinvention of Romanticism. Subjectivism of various kinds is explored in the love poems of Kvitka, the idealist philosophisings of Iurii Bedryk, the self-explorations of Neda Nezhdana, the Byronic self-idealisation of Ivan Andrusiak, and the quest for personal identity between the Ukrainianness and Russianness of Oleksandr Chekmyshev. The 'Great Themes', Death in particular, are brought out for airing. In general, pessimism is the fashion. Rudenko speaks in the foreword to *Molode vyno* of 'these Schopenhauerian times',[25] while Rozumnyi, who has the advantage of studying philosophy, is convinced in the afterword that 'being and life ... touch at one point only: death. Only death can engage the artist who seeks meaning and life simultaneously.'[26]

If post-colonialism means freedom from colonial complexes and from the compulsion to write as though the experience of colonialism is co-extensive with life itself, then the creativity of the newcomers is, indeed, post-colonial. This may – who knows? – be the first literary generation that matures without the millstone of duty to an imperative of liberation around its neck. But it is more likely that, at least as a group, these young poets are still at the point of exploring what seems available to them in literary and philosophical tradition. The essentially archival nature, the exercise quality, of their work to date suggests that their orientation in the cultural force-field left behind by colonialism has yet to come.

Notes

1. Ihor Rymaruk (ed.), *Visimdesiatnyky: Antolohiia novoi ukrains'koi poezii* (Edmonton: Canadian Institute of Ukrainian Studies Press, 1990).
2. 'Post-Colonial Features in Contemporary Ukrainian Culture', *Australian Slavonic and East European Studies*, Vol. 6, No. 2 (1992), pp. 41–55.
3. For an anthology representative of this movement up to 1992, see the special issue,

edited by Lidiia Stefanivs'ka [Stefanowska], of the journal *Zustrichi* (Warsaw), 1994, No. 1 (8).

4. For an informed discussion of the avantgardist heritage of Bu-Ba-Bu, Luhosad and Propala hramota, see Halyna Chernysh, 'Semenko brate ia tezh kudlatyi narobym dyva u svita khati', *Prapor*, 1990, No. 7, pp. 22–6; see also Natalka Bilotserkivet, 'BU-BA-BU ta in. Ukrains'kyi literaturnyi neoavanhard: Portret odnoho roku', *Slovo i chas*, 1991, No. 1, pp. 42–52; and Liubomyr Strynhaliuk, 'Apostoly antyestetyky' [on Nova deheneratsiia], *Slovo i chas*, 1993, No. 8, pp. 86–8.

5. See my article, 'Ukrainian Literature and the Erotics of Post-Colonialism', *Harvard Ukrainian Studies*, Vol. 17, Nos 1–2 (1993), pp. 110–26.

6. Iurii Mushketyk, 'Koleso: kil'ka dumok z pryvodu suchasnoho ukrains'koho post-avanhardu', *Literaturna Ukraina*, 27 October 1994, pp. 1 and 4 (p. 4).

7. *Pereval*, 1993, No. 1, p. 153.

8. Viktor Neborak, 'Henezys litaiuchoi holovy', in *Litaiucha holova* (Kyiv: Molod', 1990) p. 12.

9. Report in Olena Lohvynenko, 'Kozhen sam sobi Ariadna. Iakshcho maie svoiu nytku, to mozhe podaty ii inshym', *Literaturna Ukraina*, 26 May 1994, p. 2.

10. Volodymyr Tsybul'ko, 'Muzei: poema', in his collection *Piramida* (Zhytomyr: Zhytomyrs'kyi visnyk, 1992), p. 31.

11. Ibid., p. 31.

12. *Suchasnist'*, 1993, No. 7.

13. 'Koleso', p. 4.

14. Viacheslav Medvid', 'Zbahnuvshy, shcho nalezhyte do velykoi kul'tury, ne zakhochete dyvuvaty svit 'karnavalarny': Interv'iu z pys'mennykom zi sproboiu zanurennia u psyholohiiu tvorchosti', *Literaturna Ukraina*, 6 May 1993, p. 3.

15. Ievhen Pashkovs'kyi, 'Literatura iak zlochyn', *Osnova*, 1993, No. 2, pp. 83–8 (p. 87).

16. See my article, 'On the Possibility of Opposition Under *Glasnost*'', in Chris Worth, Pauline Nestor and Marko Pavlyshyn (eds), *Literature and Opposition* (Melbourne: Centre for Comparative Literature and Cultural Studies, Monash University, 1994), pp. 165–78.

17. Iaroslav Mel'nyk, 'Psyholohichnyi rozmovnyk: vidpovidaiut' na anketu Volodymyr Briuhhen i Iaroslav Mel'nyk', *Literaturna Ukraina*, 17 March 1994, p. 3.

18. 'Bu-Ba-Bu i vse inshe', *Literaturna Ukraina*, 28 March 1991, p. 7.

19. Iurii Andrukhovych, 'Ave, "Kraisler"!', *Suchasnist'*, 1994, No. 5, pp. 5–15 (p. 6).

20. 'Suchasna ukrains'ka literatura v konteksti dukhovnoho vidrodzhennia: Novyi vytok chy kompleks 'rozdorizhzhia'?', *Literaturna Ukraina*, 21 April 1994, p. 5.

21. 'Koleso', p. 1.

22. An exception is Tamara Hundorova's article 'Postmodernists'ka fiktsiia Andrukhovycha z postkolonial'nym znakom pytannia', *Suchasnist'*, 1993, No. 7, pp. 79–83, and her observations in 'Dekadans i postmodernizm: pytannia movy', *Svitovyd*, 1995, No. 1 (19), pp. 64–75 (p. 73). See also my article, 'Shcho peretvoriuiet'sia v "Rekreatsiiakh" Andrukhovycha', *Suchasnist'*, 1993, No. 12, pp. 115–27.

23. Viacheslav Medvid', 'Vin napysav "Marusiu": Do 160-i richnytsi pochatku drukuvannia pratvoru nashoi novoi prozy – "Marusi" Hryhoriia Kvitky-

Osnov'ianenka', *Osnova*, 1993, No. 1, pp. 120–23 (pp. 120–21).

24. Maksym Rozumnyi, 'Pid kolesom', *Literaturna Ukraina*, 1 December 1994, p. 7.

25. Serhii Rudenko, 'Ostanni proroky v kraini vchorashnikh bohiv', in *Molode vyno: Antolohiia poezii*, edited by Maksym Rozumnyi and Serhii Rudenko (Kyiv: Smoloskyp, 1994), p. 5.

26. Maksym Rozumnyi, 'Im'ia im – iliuzion', *Molode vyno*, p. 227.

3 The Problem of the Definitive Literary Text and Political Censorship

Larissa M. L. Z. Onyshkevych

When the process of writing a literary work is affected by censorship, it influences the final product and its reception. Censorship may be enforced either intrinsically or extrinsically, that is, by the writer or by an outside group or regime. The difference is especially notable when the literary work has several variants, thus creating a problem in deciding what was the author's intent and, accordingly, which version should be considered the definitive text.

Censorship is a forced intrusion by an outside element that makes an author rewrite his work, and is often manifested in the form of a political censor – an office usually functioning as a part of a centralized dictatorial and totalitarian government. Censors have no tolerance for the individualism of those who hold their own opinions (especially expressed in writing) which are contrary to the opinions of those in power. Without asking for any consensus from their citizens, dictatorial regimes or influential parties make their own ideology the legitimate and only one, and destroy or suppress all other expressions, including those in literature.[1] This in turn leads to critical situations and poignant moral choices for writers; some challenge any such intrusion into their freedom and creative process, and usually pay the price with their own freedom or lives. Other writers are more concerned that their work be saved, and are willing to keep on producing other versions until the censor is satisfied. This latter situation creates a problem for textual scholarship in determining which variant should then be considered the definitive text.

Types of Censorship

Censorship in literature may be multivalent, and is carried out in several ways: by the author who desires to improve a work artistically; by the author who attempts to heed the requirements of political censorship and therefore writes accordingly; and by means of the writer's collaboration or submission to the censors' requirements, through the production of new authorial variants of the text. The first situation is part of a natural process, and represents a type of artistic inner censorship. In the second case, the text does not need to be censored: since it was written specifically to fit the given conditions, it was pre-censored in the planning process and in a way actually represents self-censorship, with the author wishing to write one way (and perhaps even keeping a copy hidden for a freer future, whether in his or her lifetime or not), but deciding to be more pragmatic, knowing that the censors would not allow it to be published. It is a quite clear-cut situation, with no guesswork involved, since the requirements are known, the rules obeyed, and thus no official censoring intrusion is needed: the author has chosen to satisfy a specific plan. In the third case, with the presence of external censorship, the situation is quite complicated. The rules and requirements are obeyed by stages, but the censor is never quite satisfied, and the author keeps on trying until a new variant can pass the censor's test. As a result, there may be a multitude of variants, which upon initial inspection may appear to be clones. It is this latter situation which creates a problem in literary interpretation and textual analysis, and therefore requires detailed study and methodology,[2] since the existing textual scholarship does not actually deal with emendations and alterations due to political censorship.

How various literary texts were self-censored by authors may be well illustrated with examples from Ukrainian literature, although written in various situations, but under dictatorial regimes. In the nineteenth century, Ukrainian authors (who were living in that part of Ukraine which was then under Russian tsarist rule) had to police their own works if they wanted to have them published. And even then many had to pay with their freedom for what they dared to write: the leading Ukrainian poet, Taras Shevchenko (1814–61) received a ten-year sentence (signed by Tsar Nicholas I) for his poetry, and was even forbidden to write and paint during that period. Subsequently, at the turn of the century, it seemed that a more enlightened period had arrived; however, the Russian tsarist regime was particularly strict towards Ukrainian literature (several *ukases* were issued for that purpose, restricting the use of Ukrainian language). When Lesia Ukrainka (1871–1913) wrote her drama in verse *In the Wilderness*, she too was put under political pressure by the censors regarding what she could express in Ukrainian, since any allusions to Ukraine's situation within the Russian Empire would be strictly pursued and then rooted out. As a result, she hardly ever used Ukrainian settings in her plays. In order to camouflage local political and social problems of the day, she usually turned to an exotic *topos* or an earlier period, or employed old myths and legends. By studying her archives, one can uncover how she worked and what major or minor changes she made in her works.[3] However, such a creative process is quite natural, and often the definitive text is chronologically the latest one that the author makes, and, since it is a case of authorial intent due to artistic choice, it may represent a variant of an 'inner censorship'.

In the twentieth century, however, we find a much more visible external censorship *par excellence*, when authors, under duress, either independently or with the aid of editors, made significant deletions from or insertions into their texts. This highly-developed variant of self-censorship may be demonstrated in countless literary works from the Nazi period, and in particular from the seventy-year Soviet period. For example, the popular Soviet Ukrainian playwright, Ivan Kocherha (1881–1952), published both Ukrainian and Russian language editions of his plays, and in particular his *Masters of Time*, in 1934, 1938 and 1951. In the later editions, several scenes which were not complimentary to the Soviet way of life were omitted, although some of the new ones were ambiguous or confusing (whether they were complimentary or sarcastic) in reference to presentations of Soviet reality.[4]

Such examples of self-censorship allow researchers and editors to study the process of how the changes were made. Literary scholars thus become archaeologists, peeling off the palimpsests or digging for the artefacts of literature. These are then demonstrated to the public, with definitive texts representing the core of the findings. After all, such changes were made by the authors themselves, and the texts still represent some type of unity.

The third category, however, deals with a different situation. In 1994, an entire issue (Vol. 109, No. 1, January 1994) of the *Publications of the Modern Language Association* was dedicated to the subject of censorship. Michael Holquist of Yale University, in his introductory article, commented that censorship has existed since Roman times, when censors began to oversee 'public morals'. He pointed out 'a fundamental quality of censorship: its authority to prohibit can never be separated from its need to include.'[5] Later he added that 'it was the Soviet Union of the 1930s that pioneered new regions of control not only in what could not be said but also in a new area, what had to be said.'[6] Most of the articles in the issue of *PMLA*,[7] however, deal with deciphering hidden meanings, hidden layers of the palimpsests, and do not consider cases when parts of the works were replaced, resulting in an intrusively inserted, patched-up product, one that changes the faces of its protagonists or the unity and structure of its poetics, thereby creating an eclectic and artificial text.

Such a situation represents the heart of a quite different problem: when the author, under the external pressure of censorship or of a political regime, frantically keeps on changing a text, does it then become a different text, or just a variant of an earlier one? Which variant should then be considered the definitive text: the first one – while all the succeeding ones should be treated as mere substitutes? Or should one consider it a hybrid, made by reacting to given political pressures and demands? If so, should it be considered a text freely written by the author? The dilemma is a weighty one when the author can no longer be consulted.

In Soviet Ukrainian literature alone, there are countless examples of a writer attempting to save his 'child' by undertaking to do the extensive surgery himself. By attempting to save the work and the protagonist (and often his own life, too), the author creates a new text, a new protagonist – whether under a different name or not. As a result, the patched-up product would shout at a distance that it was not the original, organic creation with the same poetics or structure.

There are countless examples of such cases in Soviet literature, especially in Soviet Ukrainian literature, involving leading Ukrainian writers: Iurii Ianovskyi's *Žyva voda* (*Live Water*, 1947) had to be rewritten because it showed Russians in a negative light, and was published posthumously as *Peace* in 1956; or Oleksander Dovzhenko's renowned film *Zvenyhora* (1927), which was fated to have several variants, in the numerous attempts by Dovzhenko to please the censors and finally provide an ending which would show the communists as victors. Another example that stands out glaringly and painfully is Mykola Kulish's (1892–1937?) play, *The Sonata Pathétique*.

Kulish, an accomplished author of thirteen plays, was able to see only six of them in print, since all publication was under government control in the USSR. In 1934 he was labeled a 'nationalist', and was arrested and sentenced to ten years in a concentration camp, where he died. It is because the censors refused to allow the play in Ukraine that *Sonata Pathétique* – one of the greatest works of Ukrainian literature and an outstanding drama – has so many variants that it makes the interpretation of the text quite difficult. Each new variant turned it into a new, more taxing labyrinth.

The Case of the Play *The Sonata Pathétique*

Just what elements of his play Kulish considered important when he originally completed the play may be clearly seen from his own words (in a public discussion of the work in 1931), describing how he composed it:

> this is an attempt to introduce into dramaturgy a [specific] musical composition as an integral organic part, and not [just] an accompaniment; this is an attempt to provide a rhythmic structure for a play, from the beginning to the end; this is an attempt to structure a work on the organic ties of words, rhythm, movement, light, music.[8]

In 1930, Kulish was not able to get the censor's permission to stage this play in Ukraine. He knew that the political circle around him was growing tighter and tighter, and he worked feverishly on new variants. He wanted his child to see daylight – to see the stage – even if only in a Russian translation, and even if not in his own country, Ukraine, but in Russia.[9]

In Kulish's archives there are several versions, changes, and insertions, which the author sent to his translator, so that each translation would be made from a different variant.[10] After a number of rewrites, the play was passed, and the première took place in 1931 in Russia, in Leningrad (at the Bolshoi Dramaticheskii Theatre), and several days later, in Moscow (at the Kamernyi Theatre), where it was hailed as one of the best plays of the period.[11] Just how eager Kulish was to see his play performed can be deduced from his insistence that the translator submit to the censor each new variant of every scene. In his archives we can find countless notes from 1931, with the heading 'dramatised fragments'. During that time, he often complained how difficult it was to rewrite the play, or that he could not rewrite Act I, and that he only made a new outline for Acts II and III (out of the total of five acts).[12]

The play's publication history reflects the odyssey of Kulish's efforts: a 1932 German stage variant; a 1943 Ukrainian text published in L'viv, and then reprinted in New York in 1955; and two Soviet Ukrainian texts from 1968 and 1969, but only after the Russian version appeared first (based on the final variant translated for the Kamernyi Theatre in 1931).[13] The 1943 Ukrainian publication was based on the original version; however, since at that time Ukraine was under the Nazi occupation, several sentences were censored from the play, since otherwise some comments could have been interpreted as criticizing the Nazi regime.

The basic difference between all these texts lies in the last two acts, specifically in the ending.[14] In the 1943 text, the heroine, Maryna, admits her role as a revolutionary leader of Ukrainian partisans; in the Soviet versions she shows signs of having lost her mind, does not confess, and only wants to save her life by blaming the poet Ilko.

There are also many unpublished variants in which the author added some important insertions about the protagonists' past. In some of the later ones, he even inserted facts from Ukrainian history, and this provided some risky parallels to certain aspects of the Soviet period: 'The land was all in darkness. In such a darkness, that it even forgot its own past ... Then the land awakens. The land begins to stir. But who is going to lead it?'[15]

Among one of the most crucial changes in the last variants is the scene where the poet kills Maryna. In another variant, he even considers suicide, but then decides that it would be irresponsible. These two variants are basically similar, especially if one sees Maryna as the poet's double; the two protagonists are equally split in their aims and desires. In the final scene Maryna actually sees him as two different people. The poet describes this himself: 'She tries to look me in the eye, but at an illusionary me. You are looking at him (she points at me), at your double.' She then continues to stress this duplicity: 'Go ahead, my dear, ask your double why he has sent me here to this dark basement.' And then the poet describes the scene: 'she passes by me, as if actually being led by my double'.[16]

In the latest editions of *Sonata Pathétique*, Maryna is shown not as a person dedicated to her cause, a Ukrainian patriot and leader, but only as a selfish, deranged and even lovesick, lonely woman. The poet, meanwhile, metamorphoses from a symbol of complete devotion to Maryna, an idealist who wants to have a clear conscience and clean hands, in the end demonstrating a split personality, and, in some of the last variants, killing his former love in order to follow the communists.

Such considerably different versions changed the whole *persona* of the protagonist, Maryna. A separate methodology exists in textual scholarship for situations when changes are made during a normal authorial rewriting process. However, for literary works written in situations of severe censorship (and all the consequences that it may entail), it is extremely hard to search for the definitive text. One may need to analyse, for example, how the character of the protagonist is altered to become a completely different personality, thereby contributing to a different literary whole.

Significant changes in the Aristotelian sense of *ethos* (the social aspect of a given work, the relationship of the author to the reader), also contribute to the changes in *dianoia* (which includes the literal meaning, as well as the descriptive, formal and archetypal one, or the unity of the poetics). As a result, the work undergoes a metamorphosis in the *mythos,* the third Aristotelian component. If one analyses the elements of the original version of the play (published in 1943), *The Sonata Pathétique* may be assigned to an *apocalyptic* imagery of a myth.[17] This first version fulfils all the characteristics of this mode. The published Soviet variant is rather on the threshold of the *demonic* mythos (while the first variant only hints at it), by shifting from a tragedy to a parody, requiring a victim in order to retain the leader–tyrant position. This demonic world also requires death, which the author dutifully provided in the new versions. In the apocalyptic mythos, human *dreams and desires* are expressed; in the demonic – a different world rules, a world that no one wants; it is a sick world, full of nightmares, 'bondage and pain and confusion … ruins and catacombs',[18] an existential hell. The final scenes in the later variants (published in the Soviet editions) provide these elements. The very fact that these changes have transferred the mode of the play into another category almost makes it a different or new work of literature, thus displaying a structural disunity of imagery and mythos in the newer variants.

A similar conclusion may be drawn from the changes made in the text in relation to a musical composition:[19] originally, the play was carefully constructed on parallels to the Beethoven sonata of the same name, in both structure, mode, and atmosphere (that is why Kulish used and stressed the title, and also noted in numerous parts of the play just what part of the sonata was imagined by Ilko, or was played on the piano by Maryna, or was heard by other protagonists). For example, in the first versions, in the last act, just before the *Rondo* part (in the musical composition), there are no structural or mood divergencies between the text and the music, when drops of water (with music performed *con moto)* count time for Maryna. Both the music and the text also end with a frantic circling of a bird, and at the end the protagonist appropriately discloses her pseudonym as 'The Gull'. She then identifies herself as the gull in Ukrainian folklore, standing at the crossroads of history and being taken advantage of by the foreign passers-by. Maryna admits to being the leader of the revolutionaries and boldly faces the gallows. In the musical text, there are no hints of falsehood or madness; neither did they exist in the first variant of the text. However, the variants written for the Russian translation (which include the final discussion between the poet and Maryna, and then the killing), extend the play's text somewhat *beyond* the musical composition.[20] Had the music had at least a dozen bars more, the key and the tone would have had to be cynical, rather than frantic. These later versions of the play's ending not only provide a diametrically different interpretation of Maryna, but also a different structure and mood for the ending; it is important to note that they do not correspond to the structure and mood of Beethoven's sonata, while the first version adhered to it rigorously, since it represented a very important structural element for the play.

Conclusion

The above-mentioned examples from the play *The Sonata Pathétique* bring us back to the initial question posed: when, owing to dictatorial or totalitarian censorship, authors make significant changes in their work in order to save it, is the product still the same literary work? Is it the same child by the same parent? Is it a child from another father? Is it a new child, even when called by the same name? In such cases, which variant should be the definitive one? Which version should the general audience be reading? Only in scholarly editions can *all* the significant variants be included, at the risk of appearing similar to present-day detective plays, which provide a different ending for each performance. Some scholars hold the extreme view that, even when a text has typographical errors made by a printer, it is then a different literary work.[21] Do significant changes in a literary work allow the new variant to be called the same work, when the variant was not produced as part of the process of a natural evolution in the author's intent and design?

In a totalitarian regime, one does not have to see the actual handwriting of the censor in order to feel the results of his omnipresence in the life of a literary work or even the writer. It was a censor who did not allow *The Sonata Pathétique* to be performed in Ukraine; censors also provided the final permission to stage it in Russia. After the Chief Repertoire Committee in Kiev refused to allow the staging of the play in Ukraine, knowing that censors in Ukraine were stricter than in Russia (that is, where they did not have to watch out for 'Ukrainian nationalist deviations' and similar sins), Kulish decided to try his luck at any price there. His translator, Pavel Zienkevich, gave the translation to Alexander Tairov, producer of the Moscow Kamernyi Theatre, who was very excited by the play and eager to stage it. Still, the play first had to pass the Russian Repertoire Committee and censors; thus Kulish kept on rewriting the play until a variant was accepted by that committee (which, besides making artistic choices, also performed political pre-sifting for the censor).[22] The censor's presence was pervasive, forcing Kulish to remould and redirect his work. This hovering power of censorship is felt throughout the author's frantic attempts at providing his play with even a short life.

However, it thereby creates a new problem. When, in order to satisfy a censor, the author rewrites his literary creation countless times, changing the unity and poetics of the work (which was important to Kulish), is the product still the same literary work as the one written originally? And then, after the writer's death and the end of a particular totalitarian regime, which text should one consider as the critical text? In the subsequent variants of *The Sonata Pathétique*, not only are the endings different, showing the opposing sides as victors, the protagonists' characters and integrity are different, too, creating almost a new play, and creating confusion regarding the play's appreciation and reception. In such situations the ontology of the text is extremely difficult to unravel.

Political censorship has produced literary self-censorship and has provoked authors to perform 'surgery' on their own texts, leaving scholars with the problem of searching for and choosing a definitive version. How should this be done? For works which have demonstrated a certain unity in the first or original variant, one method of pursuing this may be by searching for such unity in the other variants, for example, the unity of archetypal myths and imagery, or the parallelism with a musical composition, as demonstrated in the case of *The Sonata Pathétique*.

New approaches and perhaps a specific hermeneutics need to be developed by textual scholarship in order to allow scholars to interpret the different variants of such texts and their contexts. In order to help uncover an author's teleological design which has become either camouflaged, dissolved or buried in successive variants of a text, new discursive analyses and new criticism are needed to deal with the results of society's or history's intrusion into the fate of a literary work.

Notes

1. Michael Holquist notes that official censorship was introduced by the Romans, who used it to keep an eye on public morals: see his 'Corrupt Originals: The Paradox of Censorship', *Publications of Modern Language Association*, January 1994, p. 15.
2. The problem of having different variants became obvious as early as the tenth century, when several versions of old manuscripts surfaced. In the West, a certain theoretical approach to such manuscripts has been taken in terms of changes within the texts, unintentional mistakes, and spelling or orthography of the texts of earlier periods. Of course, numerous copies, and intended and unintended changes made while transcribing, produced variant texts, often not related to any censorship.

Editors and transcribers had to deal with the editing of Shakespeare's plays, and since the end of the nineteenth century were developing a methodology for this purpose. A similar approach was taken by academic editors of the works of the leading nineteenth-century Ukrainian poet, Taras Shevchenko. However, since the 1930s, his works, in order to conform to Soviet ideology, were heavily censored. So many variants were created that scholars now have to rely on pre-Soviet and Western publications of Shevchenko in order to unravel the author's original version.

3. For example, *In the Wilderness* was initially to be called 'Richard', then 'Sculptor', and the protagonists changed accordingly: see Larissa Onyshkevych, 'Sprava vyboru v Rychardovim ekzystentsiialistychnim shukanni v *U Pushchi* Lesi Ukrainky', *Lesia Ukrainka: 1871–1971* (Philadelphia: Permanent Conference on Ukrainian Studies, 1971–1980), pp. 199–206.

4. In the 1938 edition, there were some even more critical comments on Soviet life than those published in 1934. Also, for quite a while, censors and critics did not know how to interpret the very title *Masters of Time* – whether this was a positive or negative comment, especially when at the end, former heroes and revolutionaries become chicken farmers, and 'masters' of the new, Soviet, times; or how to deal with the description that a train from Kyiv (Kiev) to Paris had to go via Moscow: see Larissa Onyshkevych. '*Hodynnykar i kurka* abo *Maistry Chasu*', *Suchasnist*, 1967, No. 1, pp. 74–82.

5. Holquist, 'Corrupt Originals', pp. 1 and 14. He also points out that '[o]ne of the ironies that define censorship as a paradox is that it predictably creates sophisticated audiences. The reader of a text known to be censored cannot be naive, if only because the act of interdiction renders a text parabolic.'

6. Ibid., p. 15.

7. Peter Scott, 'Censorship, Reading, and Interpretation: A Case Study from the Soviet Union'; Claire Cavanagh, 'Rereading the Poet's Ending: Mandelstam, Chaplin, and Stalin', in ibid.

8. From a 1931 publication, quoted in Mykola Kulish, *Tvory*, edited by Les' Taniuk (Kyiv: Dnipro, 1990), Vol. II, p. 478.

9. Neither was it published in Russian until 1960, from the Kamernyi Theatre translation variant.

10. Kulish, in one of his letters to the translator Pavel Zienkevich, mentions that, together with the director Alexander Tairov, he planned another ending for the play, but after completing it, he saw that it did not fit in with the rest.

11. It ran there for several months until May 1934, and had 43 performances, until an anonymous review threatened that the play was a cover-up for political deviations; the closing of the play was noted even in New York: 'Soviet Suppresses Play Hailed as Artistic Find', *The New York Herald–Tribune*, 15 May 1932.

12. 'I don't have the strength and time any more to work on it. This variant too was made with unbelievable difficulty...': Mykola Kulish, letter to Pavel Zienkevich, February 1931. Archives of Mykola Kulish, Manuscript Division, Institute of Literature, The National Academy of Sciences of Ukraine, Kyiv, Fund 148/471, p. 14; see also Fund 148/61, pp. 54–61, note on the cover of a new variant, n.d.

13. When George Luckyj translated the play into English, he used the Soviet variants:

George S. N. and Moira Luckyj, translators; the play was published by Ukrainian Academic Press (Littleton, CO, 1975). Les' Taniuk, in the complete edition of Kulish's plays (Kyiv, 1990), has for the first time published several variants, including even the one in which Ilko kills Maryna.

14. The plot of the play is based on events in 1917–18, with several historical forces colliding in Ukraine: Ukrainian patriots who want an independent country, Russian tsarist forces attempting to hold the Russian Empire, and communists wanting to build the Soviet Union. Maryna leads the first group. In the original variant Maryna courageously faces the scaffold when the communists uncover her. In the changed later variants, she is shown as selfish, while Ilko, the poet, goes over to the communists and hands her over to them; in other variants, he shoots her himself.

15. An added 1931 variant to Act II, Scene 3. Archives of Mykola Kulish, Manuscript Division, Institute of Literature, The National Academy of Sciences of Ukraine, Kyiv, Fund 148/66, p. 2.

16. Ibid., 148/61: 56. With reference to the image of the protagonists' doubling and split representation in the play, see Larissa Zales'ka Onyshkevych, 'Kulish i Brekht' samosposterezhennia heroia i samosposterezhennia avtora', *Suchasnist*, 1992, No. 1, pp. 131–5.

17. According to the system developed by Northrop Frye: see 'Theory of Archetypal Meaning (1): Apocalyptic Imagery', in his *Anatomy of Criticism* (Princeton, NJ: Princeton University Press, 1963), pp. 141–6. For a discussion associated with the mythos and its imagery, centred upon the word *omphalos* or the image of Easter, see Larissa Onyshkevych, 'Omphalos' u *"Patetychnii sonati"* Mykoly Kulisha', *Suchasnist*, 1994, No. 1, pp. 125–36; and Larissa Zales'ka Onyshkevych, 'Rol' Velykodnia u *Patetychnii sonati* Mykoly Kulisha', *Slovo i chas*, 1991, No. 9 (369), pp. 48–53.

18. Northrop Frye, 'Theory of Archetypal Meaning (2): Demonic Imagery', in his *Anatomy of Criticism*, p. 147.

19. I have dealt with this in depth in other publications and presentations: Larissa Onyshkevych, 'Sonata Pathétique', in *Existentialism in Modern Ukrainian Drama* (Ann Arbor, MI: University Microfilms, 1974), pp. 85–9; Larissa M.L.Z. Onyshkevych, 'Ingenuity versus Modernization: Kulish and Kostetzky', in A. Donskov and R. Sokoloski (eds), *Slavic Drama: The Question of Innovation* (Ottawa: Legas Productions, 1991), p. 138.

20. When Kulish was writing the first version, he had his daughter repeatedly play the sonata on the piano; the new variants were written without this assistance: see Antonina Kulish, 'Spohady pro Mykoly Kulisha', in Mykola Kulish, *Tvory* (New York: Ukrainian Academy of Arts and Sciences, 1955), p. 411.

21. Rene Wellek and Austin Warren, 'The Mode of Existence of a Literary Work of Art', *Theory of Literature* (New York: Harcourt, Brace & World, 1956), p. 145.

22. On 8 February 1931 Mykola Kulish wrote to Pavel Zienkevich that he was sending him a new variant of the play and asked that the 'repertoire committee' be informed about it: Mykola Kulish Archives, Fund 148/471, p. 2. On 17 October 1931 the author wrote again that he was sending the third version to Moscow, after making 'important changes': 'I think that now we can send the play to other theatres ... to the Repertoire Committee of the Kamernyi Theatre in Moscow':

Mykola Kulish Archives, Fund 148/474, p. 2. In a letter written the following day, he complains that the Repertoire Committee 'is silent for six months already' (probably referring to previous variants): Kulish Archives, Fund 148/475. The play was approved by the Main Repertoire Committee, with some changes, according to Zienkevich's letter of 17 December 1930 to Ie. Chesniekov of the Leningrad Bolshoi Dramaticheskii Theatre: Fund 148/380. After the Committee approved the changes, it was sent to the censor (Zienkevich's letter of 23 February 1931 to Chesniekov: Fund 148/382), and was approved and was staged and ran for several months in both Moscow and Leningrad, to huge critical acclaim. Then an anonymous politically critical review stopped performances until the late 1960s.

4 Transcarpathian Ukrainian Literature in the Twentieth Century

Lubica Babotová

The development of Transcarpathian Ukrainian literature[1] in the twentieth century – particularly in the early decades – is a very complicated phenomenon that has yet to be examined in depth. There is a dearth of bibliographies of published works, monographic studies, and general surveys of particular literary issues.[2] There is no doubt that the development of Transcarpathian Ukrainian literature was complicated by the turbulent and significant social and political changes taking place in twentieth-century Europe, including the area of the Transcarpathian territory: emigration; the First World War; the break-up of the Austro-Hungarian Empire; the formation of Czechoslovakia; the formation of Carpathian Rus' and Carpathian Ukraine; the Second World War; the addition of the Carpathian Ukraine to the Ukrainian Soviet Socialist Republic; the break-up of the USSR; and the recent formation of independent Ukraine and Slovakia. All these changes led to the development of various opportunities (and in some cases lack of opportunities) for the growth of cultural life.

Before the break-up of the Austro-Hungarian Empire in 1918, Transcarpathian literature was continuing and, one can even say, following the traditions of the so-called 'generation of awakeners' ('buditel'ska pokolinnya'). Up to the final days of their lives, the writers Yevgen Fentsyk (b. 1903), Ivan Syl'vai (b. 1904), and Oleksandr Mytrak (b. 1913) were actively participating in the literary process. Under backward political, economic and cultural conditions, and with an underdeveloped school system, the 'generation of awakeners' emphasised national culture as the most important weapon in the struggle for the nation's survival. For this reason the 'awakeners' devoted increased attention to didactic and educational activities and to raising national awareness. They considered national literature one of the most precise indicators of the nation's existence, and they expressed their views and intentions from the perspective of educational ideals and moral directives, not going beyond the framework of everyday life.

First and foremost, these writers proposed to their readers a didactic literature, with its own specific artistic mode of expression; but at the same time, they did not limit themselves in their criticism of the social order of the time. At the end of the nineteenth century, writers tended to pay increasing attention to the element of entertainment in their works in order to attract the attention of a broader reading public. By the first years of the twentieth century, the 'generation of awakeners' had in essence ceased its activity. The only exception was Feodosii Zlots'kyi (1846–1926), who had been published since 1867, and who reflected all the tendencies of the literary development in Transcarpathian Ukraine at that time.

At the turn of the century, new names appeared in Transcarpathian literature (Grigorii Bondar, Viktor Lehesa, Julii Chuchka, Hiador Strypskyi, Ivan Myhalka, Sydir Bilak, Vasyl' Matiatskov, Irina Nevyts'ka, and a group of writers most likely writing under pseudonyms: De Hvasteiov, Ugryn, Mykhailo T'miak and others). Writers of the new generation, unlike their predecessors, came from a different position in their socio-political world-views and gradually took a leading role in literary development. Not only did the style of literary works change, but the targeted readership changed as well. The literary practice of the time testified to the effectiveness and popularity of colloquial speech, which was gradually utilised not only by young writers, but frequently by writers of the older generation as well. This was not merely one of the signs of mutual effort, it was also an indication of the approaching new cultural epoch. While the attitudes of certain important cultural figures towards the local dialects and colloquial language varied, as early as the beginning of the twentieth century a distinct view was formed: 'scholars call our language "malorusskyi" ("Little Russian"), in order to distinguish it from "velykorusskyi" ("Great Russian"), or "maskal's'kyi" ("Moscovite"); and in order to distinguish it from Belorussian, these scholars also call our language Ukrainian–Russian'.[3]

In examining the above-mentioned problems, one may generally posit that in their works writers focused on a range of issues: the unity of the Slavic nation; the re-creation of ancient and modern history; transatlantic emigration; the image of the exploiting class; social problems of the village close to the Transcarpathian reader; and, primarily, the critical–realistic depiction of the village. They also devoted increasing attention to national patriotism. This patriotic tendency was stimulated by the Hungarian government's increasingly emboldened attempts at denationalisation (the school laws of Albert Apponi in 1907 and 1909 directed against Slavic and Romanian schools; the prohibition in 1916 against the use of primers in schools; and the directive to use the Latin alphabet instead of Cyrillic in the periodical press). Besides the writers' emphasis on patriotism, there was an increased interest in oral folk literature (Mykhailo Vrabel'), the reworking of folklore elements (Julii Chuchka, Havryiil Turianyn), and the depiction of the everyday problems faced by the nation's masses. This inspiration found in folk culture was similar to the directions taken in other literatures of that time: in Ukrainian literature (in all Ukrainian territories), Slovak, Hungarian, Polish, Russian and others. Literary activities of this kind were directed first and foremost towards preserving the uniqueness of popular culture and reacting against the people's denationalisation.

Publishing opportunities were insignificant, and limited, in effect, to the Uzhgorod newspaper *Nauka* (*Science*) (in the period 1897–1922, its name was in flux), the Budapest weekly *Nedylia* (*Sunday*) (1898–1919), and various thematic calendars (this does not include those school textbooks and religious publications that were published by the joint-stock company 'UNIO'). From that time on, only short literary genres were developed. Poems were the most frequent literary form, followed by publications of folk literature, and then short stories. Compared with the previous period, the number of dramas that were written at that time saw a sharp decrease, and even the few that were published were quite weak. According to existing information, neither longer narrative works nor novels were published. Even though some scholars have been critical in their evaluations of the Transcarpathian Ukrainian literature of the period, it is necessary, however, to give full credit to the fact that on the pages of Transcarpathian literature were published literary works that not only influenced national awareness, but also served the purpose of unifying the Ruthenians from a wider range of Ukrainian territories. Authors from the Boikiv, Lemkiv and Bachka regions, even authors from the United States, published their works in the periodicals mentioned above. Emilii Kubek, who emigrated to the United States in 1904, was for many years working with other cultural figures of his native land. He was the author of the first original novel in Transcarpathian Ukrainian literature. That novel, *Marko Sholtys. Roman iz Zhittia Podkarpatskoi Rusi (Marko Sholtys: A Novel from the Life of Subcarpathian Rus')*, after certain complications was published in the American journal *Sokil (Falcon)* in serial form in 1920. It was published as a book in 1922, in Scranton, Pennsylvania, in the United States.[4]

From the significant number of authors who entered the realm of literature before 1918, and who then influenced the formation of the Transcarpathian literary process, we should in the first place mention Iryna Nevyts'ka, Vasyl' Hrengzha-Donskyi, Luka Dem'ian and Antonii Bobul'skyi.[5] And we should not omit the most productive collector of all the Uzhgorod chronicles of the first decades of the twentieth century, Irynei Lehez (1861–1922). The works of Transcarpathian writers were influenced to a great degree by major works of Russian literature (Tolstoy, for example), translations from Hungarian and Slovak, and the extremely popular works frequently published in Transcarpathian periodicals, and authored by Stepan Rudans'kyi, Marko Vovchok, Taras Shevchenko, Ivan Franko and Bohdan Lepkyi. Almost all more or less well-known Transcarpathian writers at the beginning of their literary careers recorded folklore works and collected songs, fairy tales and proverbs, which they later used in their writing. Later, authors became more specialised in their styles (they did not write in all genres, like writers of the previous period). It is reasonable to agree with Volodymyr Hnatiuk, who stated that at the turn of the century the Transcarpathian Ukrainian ethnic territory experienced a kind of national renaissance.[6]

This renaissance was fully expressed in Subcarpathian Rus' immediately after the formation of Czechoslovakia. A positive aspect of this renaissance was that the typical problems associated with the nascent period of a national literature surfaced, as did those problems which until that time, owing to circumstances in the society, had remained in the background. The problem of a literary language and general cultural (and political) orientations became topical once again. What took place in Subcarpathian Rus' was analogous to what happened in Galicia in the 1860s, and, among other things, was probably the achievement of Galician emigrants (of Ukrainian and Russian orientation, according to widely accepted terminology). During the first phases of the formation of a national literature, the use of two languages can often be found: for example, in Norwegian, Czech, Slovak and Ukrainian literature. Subcarpathian Rus' was no exception in this respect. According to the famous Czech scholar Antonin Hartl, the literary language in Subcarpathian Rus' was 'Ukrainian or Russian, or at the very least a vernacular dialect refined by either Ukrainian or Russian'.[7] Accordingly, the literature of that time dealt with Russian and Ukrainian orientations. Each group had its own newspapers and professional journals. Periodicals of the Ukrainian orientation were in the business of publishing not only works by local authors and emigrant writers, but also the works of the Bachka Ruthenian Havryiil Kostel'nik and of Emilii Kubek from America.

Such authors as Vasyl' Hrendzha-Donskyi, Julii Borshosh-Kum'iats'kiy, Luka Dem'ian, Oleksandr Markush, Mykolai Bozhuk, Marko Barabol', Mykola Rishko, Diodnizii Zubryts'kyi, and Iryna Nevyts'ka were representatives of the Ukrainian (or national) orientation. Nevyts'ka was the author of the first historical Transcarpathian Ukrainian novel *Pravda pobidyla* (*Truth was Victorious*), which was written using Henryk Sienkiewicz's *Quo Vadis* as a model. *Truth was Victorious* was published in the newspaper *Rusin* (*The Ruthenian*) in serial form in 1923, and appeared as a book in 1924 in Priashiv. Ivan Myhalka (b. 1862) and Ivan Vas'ko (b. 1889) were the older writers of the Ukrainian orientation. Poets of this group, who initially began by writing in the folk-song tradition, moved on to love lyrics and social and everyday issues and patriotic themes with the tendencies associated with the 'awakeners'. In the 1920s and 1930s, individual tendencies began to appear in the works of the youngest representatives of the Ukrainian orientation. These tendencies were supported by the talent of particular writers and later became the foundation of what was valued in literature. However, this group would not be complete if we did not mention the emigrant writers from other Ukrainian regions: Mariika Pidhirianka, Vasyl Pachovskyi, Spyrydon Cherkasenko, and, most importantly, the most distinguished poet of the Priashiv region, Sebastiian Sabola (Zoreslav), who was well known for his profound thinking, his individual intellectual poetics, and his refined versification techniques.

Unlike the representatives of the Ukrainian orientation, the writers of the Russian orientation inherited the traditions of such great Russian writers as Aleksandr Kol'tsov, Aleksandr Pushkin, Nikolai Gogol' and Sergei Esenin. The most outstanding representatives of this group were Andrii Karabelesh, Mikhailo Popovych, Pavlo Fedor, Omelian Balets'kyi, Antonii Bobul'skyi (who used a vernacular dialect, but considered himself a writer of the Russian orientation), and the emigrants O. Popov, and Dmytro Verhun. During the 1930s, Andrii Patrus-Karpats'kyi and Fedir Ivanchov were members of the Russian-language orientation as well, but subsequently started to write in Ukrainian.

The goals of these two groups were diametrically opposed. The Ukrainian group was trying to find a path to the people. The Russian group wanted to merge with great Russian literature, to become an integral part of it, and did not want to become a provincial literature. Typical, although not original for that group, is a quotation from Mykola Homichkov, a nineteenth-century Transcarpathian activist, to the effect that 'everywhere literature is being written for the masters'. This group, however, was distant from the people, and was writing primarily for the intelligentsia (the question of what they could contribute and what they in turn received remains open). In both groups, patriotic lyrics with an 'awakening' tendency were seen as more important, but they were based on different material. The two groups differed in their understanding of national identity, both in their point of departure and in their ideological orientation. The more secular Ukrainian group argued for the integrity of the Ukrainian nation, while the more religious, abstract–conservative Russian group, with its passive messianic tendencies, believed in a 'single, undivided' Russian nation. If, before the First World War, the main goal for writers was to sustain national awareness, in the inter-war period the authors devoted more attention to the substance and content of this awareness. The struggle and chaos of that time were intensified by national social conditions and by various political tendencies. At that time, open pro-Moscow and pro-Ruthenian sentiments, which later became pro-Hungarian sentiments, complicated not only the political, but also the cultural and social situation of the nation's populace.

After the Second World War, the Ukrainian ethnic territory that previously belonged to Hungary and had always been under the rule of one government was divided between two states. It comes as no surprise that this fact exerted a noticeable influence on the development of literature. Carpathian Ukraine became part of the USSR, while the Priashiv region was still within the borders of Czechoslovakia. In both countries, the Communist Party, which already had strong support in Transcarpathia and in the Priashiv region as early as the inter-war period, assumed a leading role. The stronger group of talented writers stayed in the USSR. The literary traditions in Eastern Slovakia remained much weaker. Gradually, it became obvious that the absence of a cultural environment which would stimulate the development of literature and become its trustworthy consumer had an adverse affect on the emergence and development of the literature of the Ukrainians of Czechoslovakia. The first efforts to adapt to the new reality by means of the poetic word were observable in the USSR and Czechoslovakia immediately after the war. Their creative output, however, for the most part lacked a clear sense of purpose, and did not have an expressly defined literary aesthetic ideal. And in the works of weaker writers, it often translated into encomiastic tendencies.

After the war, poetry was the dominant trend of the literature of the Czechoslovakian Ukrainians, while prose emerged only in the 1950s. The Ukrainian writers in Czechoslovakia discussed only regional problems in their works; local patriotism and a provincial quality were prevalent features. Only much later did the authors begin to overcome these limitations.

After the repression in 1968 of the 'Prague spring', literature came under strict state control, and the only writers allowed to be published limited their works to the themes of Lenin, Party, the USSR, Communism, and so on. After a certain time, the best authors were able to stop using formulaic approaches in their works and were able to enter into a broader literary context (Ivan Matsynskyi, Josyf Zbiglei, Stefan Hostiniak). As far as language is concerned, these writers used the Ukrainian literary language (some of them stopped using the Russian language in the 1950s). At the same time, the works of 'folk writers' using the local dialect saw publication.

The situation in Soviet Transcarpathia was somewhat different. The authors had a wide reading public. However, in Soviet Transcarpathia, as in Czechoslovakia, the most recognised writers were those who were writing in the official genre of so-called 'Socialist Realism', describing with great enthusiasm the social life of that time, one-sidedly castigating the old ways, and reflecting the struggle for shining communist ideals. In the post-war period, all literary genres were developed, small and large epic works appeared, and the thematic range of works increased.

Despite a certain usage of cliché, and despite the fact that the writers' output was financially stimulated, and therefore controlled, Ukrainian literature was enriched by a number of talented new authors: Pavlo Tsybul'skyi, Jurii Kerekesh, Ivan Chendei, Petro Ugliarenko, Ivan Dolgosh, Petro Skunts' and others.

The changes which took place after the break-up of the Communist bloc have their pluses and minuses. Among the pluses is the freedom of speech; among the minuses is the new and unfavourable economic situation for writers. Problems have begun to appear that are new to readers, and which sometimes have a political subtext. But only the future can reveal what truly positive aspects these changes will bring to the literary development of twentieth-century Transcarpathian literature.

> *Translated from the Ukrainian by Vadim Marchuk,*
> *Anatoly Vishevsky and Todd Patrick Armstrong*

Notes

1. The term 'Transcarpathian Ukrainian literature' is used to specify the literature of the 'rusini' ('Ruthenians' – the historical name of Ukrainians who lived in the Austrian Empire, and later in Austro-Hungary), who were born on the territories of present Eastern Slovakia (Priashiv region) and the Transcarpathian (Zakarpats'koi) region of the Ukraine.
2. Among the most important studies which have to some degree touched on this subject – from different specific ideological perspectives – are the following: N. Lelekach 'Podkarpatskoe pys'menstvo na pochatku XX veka', *Zoria*, 1943, Nos 1–4, pp. 229–57; P.M. Lisovyi, 'Ukraiins'ka literatura v zakarpats'kii periodyci (kinets' XIX – pochatok XX st.)', *Radiants'ke literaturoznavstvo*, Vol. 14, No. 10 (1970), pp. 34–40; Mykytas' V., *Z nochi probyvalys'* ... (Uzhgorod, 1977); D.N. Vergun, 'Karpato-Russkaya literatura', in D.N. Vergun, *Vosem' lektsii o Podkarpatskoi Rusi* (Prague, 1925), pp. 47–60; A. Hartl, *Literární obrození podkarpatských Rusínů v letech 1920–1930* (Prague, 1930); Ju. Balega,

Literatura Zakarpattia dvadtsiatyx-tridtsiatyx rokiv XX stolittia (Kiev, 1962); *Khudozlnii vidkruttya cly pravda faktu?* (Uzhgorod, 1969); E. Nedzel'skyi, *Ocherk karpatorusskoi literatury* (Uzhgorod, 1932); S. Bonkálo, *A Káepátalii rutén irodalom és müvelödés* (Pécs, 1935); V. Birchak, *Literaturni stremlinnia podkarpats'koi Rusy*, 2nd edn (Uzhgorod, 1937); *Istoriia podkarpatorus'koi literatury* (Ungvar, 1942); O. Grabar', *Poeziia Zakarpat'ia 1939–1944* (Bratislava, 1957); V. Pop, *Strumku velikoii riky* (Uzhgorod, 1961); I. Vyshnevs'kyi, *Traditsiii ta suchasnist'* (L'viv, 1963); E. Pelens'kyi, 'Pys'menstvo', in *Karpats'ka Ukraiina, geografiia-istoriia-kul'tura* (New York, 1972), pp. 108–121; Y. Voloshchuk, *Sovremennaia ukrainskaia literatura v Chekhoslovakii* (Bratislava, 1957); Orest Zilynskyi (ed.), *Literatura chekhoslovats'kykh ukraiintsiv v 1945-1967* (Priashiv, 1968); J. Sirka, *The Development of Ukrainian Literature in Czechoslovakia 1945–1975* (Frankfurt-am-Main, 1978); *Rozvytok natsional'noii svidomosti lemkiv Priashivshchyny u svitli ukraiins'koii khudozhn'yoi literartury Chekhoslovachchyny* (Munich, 1980); K. Rosenbaum (ed.), *Ukraiinská literatúra v ChSSR* (Bratislava, 1981); M. Roman, *Shliakhi literatury ukrainciv Chekhoslovachchyny pislia 1945* (Pryashiv, 1978); *Literatura i chas* (Priashiv, 1986); F. Kovach, *Dialogy* (Priashiv, 1988).

3. I. Bunganich, 'Russkii iazyk', *Nauka* (Uzhgorod) 4 June 1903, pp. 11, 5.

4. Emilii Kubek, 'Materialy do Slovnika kul'tury ukraiinciv Chekhoslovachchyny', *Duklia* (Priashiv), item 37, 1989, No. 1, pp. 76–7.

5. Critics have not failed to appraise the first three of the writers mentioned. Of A. Bobul'skyi one can learn most from an article by Bohdan Marets', 'Bobul'skyi Antonii. Materialy do Slovnika kul'tury ukraiinciv Chekhoslovachchyny', *Duklia* (Priashiv), item 36, 1988, No. 4, p. 75.

6. V. Hnatiuk, 'Rusíni v Uhrách', in Adolf Cherný (ed.), *Slovanský přehled. Slovník statí, dopisův a zpráv ze zhivota slovanského*, Roch. I (Prague: 1899), pp. 216–22,; 418–27.

7. Hartl, *Literární obrození podkarpatských Rusínů*, p. 3.

5 Poetry and Politics
The New Wave and György Petri

George Gömöri

There are moments and, indeed, periods in the history of modern Polish and Hungarian literature which are difficult to comprehend outside their social and political contexts. And there is hardly any time in the recent past when politics played such an important structural (that is, aesthetics-shaping) role in poetry as the year 1968, a year of rebellion and confrontation throughout Europe. In this essay I should like to draw a comparison between the poetic maturing of the Polish movement loosely named 'Nowa Fala' (New Wave) and the appearance of a force of poetic protest in Hungary, named György Petri. In doing so I shall try to highlight the central role of language (the validity of which is strenuously denied by many post-modernists), a role which was acknowledged at the time by both participants and critics of these politically influenced literary developments.

First of all, what constituted the New Wave? In an essay written many years later Zbigniew Bieńkowski stated that it was 'neither an artistic school nor an historical event'.[1] This is a statement which needs clarification. True, the New Wave (which, incidentally, was sometimes dubbed the 'generation of confrontationists', if that is how we translate *kontestatorzy)* did not produce artistic manifestos *à la* Peiper and Przyboś; neither did it arise as a result of a single historical event. But by the early 1970s it did have its 'poetics' and, as we stated at the beginning, the events of 1968–70 – but mainly 1968 – played a decisive role in the formulation of that poetic theory. And while the first theoretical formulation came from the pen of Stanisław Barańczak and Ryszard Krynicki in 1971 – I am referring, of course, to the often-quoted *Nieufni i zadufani* (*The Mistrustful and the Presumptuous*) – the poetic practice characteristic of the New Wave was already clearly illustrated earlier, in books of poems such as *Jednym tchem* (*In One Breath*) and *Organizm zbiorowy* (*Collective Organism*) by Barańczak and Krynicki respectively. I think the poems here were more

47

important than the theory; at any rate, when putting together their book of critical essays which was published by Ossolineum, neither critic could speak completely unhampered – censorship was a restraining factor. So in a sense the attacks of the 'new romantics' against 'petrified neo-classicism' and advocacy of the 'linguistic school' in preference to such heterogeneous groups as the semi-conformist rebels of *Współczesność* (*Contemporary Life*) camouflaged political rather than generational differences.

What was new in the poems and theoretical views of these two Poznań poets can be expressed in one sentence: they took language seriously. The atmosphere of post-war Poland was surrealistic – for many years, certainly until 1956, language was used to camouflage rather than to define reality. Most newspapers and broadcasts were written in something close to Orwellian 'Newspeak' (or, in Polish, *nowomowa*), whereas people communicated in everyday life in a different, more normal language. Tadeusz Nyczek, a critic belonging to this generation, remembering his childhood writes about 'the double-language of officialdom and non-officialdom'[2] which surreptitiously became an organic part of the mentality of young people who grew up in 'People's Poland'. While the changes of October 1956 stopped the necessity of using Doublethink and Doublespeak in all circumstances, they did not remove the linguistic straitjacket from society as a whole; they only created areas of relative autonomy within which one could pretend to speak as one wanted. So, for example, in literature one could now 'experiment', so long as one did not question the hegemony of the communist party or the supremacy of Marxist philosophy. Allegories were tolerated, for only intellectuals bothered to read and decipher allegories. The press and the media remained in the safe hands of trusted *apparatchiks* and skilful fellow-travellers.

The constraints of this compromise became increasingly clear in the mid-1960s. After Leszek Kolakowski's famous lecture at Warsaw University in 1966 and the political repercussions that followed, a large number of intellectuals, writers and artists alike, left the PZPR (the Polish United Workers' Party, or communist party). But it was only the banning of Mickiewicz's *The Forefathers' Eve Part III* and the brutally suppressed student demonstrations that followed in March 1968 which finally revealed the true face of the 'post-Stalinist' regime. The armed intervention of Warsaw Pact countries in Czechoslovakia in the summer of the same year once again demonstrated the imperialist nature of Soviet-type communism and showed that ultimately the system could not be reformed. Because of this 1968 became a watershed in the life of many young people in Poland.

Barańczak and Krynicki, to be sure, had been critical of the system years earlier. They could see how the regime, through the newspapers and the media, manipulated public opinion, thereby constantly creating a false reality – or rather unreality – which isolated individual Poles from one another, filled them with fear, or both simultaneously. 'German revanchism' was one of these sinister slogans; in 1968 'Zionist conspiracy' became another. At any rate, as more brutal forms of coercion became inapplicable (although truncheons were used against student demonstrators as much in socialist Warsaw as in capitalist Paris) the control of the language gained importance. This is why Barańczak would believe (and stresses in *Nieufni and zadufani*) that experimentation with the language could change the 'equilibrium of the world.'[3] Krynicki sees language as a factor which 'rigidifies' reality, and he states that the role of poet is to set reality free from this stultification. According to him, linguistic poetry can renew the world.[4]

The 'linguists' of Poznań were soon joined by some poets of the Cracow group 'Teraz' ('Now'), notably Adam Zagajewski and Julian Kornhauser. Their book *Świat nieprzedstawiony* (*The Undescribed World*) in a sense completed the theoretical barrage of Barańczak and Krynicki by attacking the narrow aestheticism and escapism of the previous generation. Their programme (which, in the words of the older critic Bieńkowski, was characterised by 'laudable imprecision') postulated a directness of expression, a concreteness, the main slogan being 'direct speech' ('mówienie wprost').[5] And the aim of the poet is not necessarily to restore the true meaning of words but to achieve a cognition of 'full and real life'.[6] In this respect, Zagajewski's attitude to 'officialese' is similar to that of the Poznań poets, and the tool he uses to destroy the reign of *nowomowa* is the same that is used by his colleagues: irony. The consistent application of irony, of course, is not new in modern Polish poetry, but while Zbigniew Herbert's or Wisława Szymborska's irony is more historically and culturally grounded, that of the New Wave focuses on the abuses and distortions of the language.

It is here appropriate to give a few examples of poems representative of the New Wave written between 1967 and 1971. Stanisław Barańczak's 'Spójrzmy prawdzie w oczy' ('Let's look truth in the eyes') is simply a string of images and metaphors, variants on the word 'oczy' ('eyes'), the poet taking literally the official slogan: 'Let's look truth in the eyes':

> Spójrzmy prawdzie w oczy: w nieobecne
> oczy potrąconego przypadkowo
> przechodnia z podniesionym kołnierzem; w stężałe
> oczy wzniesione ku tablicy z odjazdami
> dalekobieżnych pociągów; w krótkowzroczne
> oczy wpatrzone z bliska w gazetowy petit ...
>
> (Let's look truth in the eyes: in the absent
> eyes of an accidentally jostled
> pedestrian with an upturned collar; in the intense
> eyes turned up towards the departure times
> of long-distance trains; in the short-sighted
> eyes peering closely at the newspaper small print ...)[7]

Barańczak's poetic technique was described by Włodzimierz Bolecki as based on the 'principle of amplification'.[8] Very often standard, everyday speech is taken out of context and by being turned into a metaphor elevated into a poetic language. In other cases not only official language but other forms of official communication such as a questionnaire are parodied, as for example in the excellent 'Wypełnić czytelnym pismem ...' ('Complete in legible writing ...').[9]

Adam Zagajewski's third collection was published in 1979, and the following quotation comes from that book, although the poem itself was written in the early 1970s:

> Jeśli żyjesz w państwie deficytowym,
> w którym wielka ilość przemówień
> równoważy wszystkie niedomówienia,
> w którym ogrody botaniczne i zielniki
> są wzorem poprawności językowej ...

> (If you live in a loss-making country
> where the large number of official speeches
> equals all things only hinted at,
> in which botanical gardens and herbaria
> are models of linguistic correctness ...)[10]

Zagajewski is less interested in linguistic parody than Barańczak, but his attitude to the half-truths and glib assertions of the press and media is equally scornful. None the less, in later years his interest in 'historicism' made him move away from the language-centredness of the New Wave.

By 1974, one could look back on the New Wave as something that had happened in the past; it was then that Stanisław Barańczak (who is as good a critic as a poet can possibly be) tried to sum up the shared characteristics of the movement, apart from such obvious ones as 'they were united only in negation'. This he did in his essay 'Pokolenie 68: próba przedwczesnego bilansu' ('Generation 68: An Attempt at a Premature Reckoning'), later reprinted in the collection *Etyka i poetyka (Ethics and Poetics)*.[11] First he stated quite bluntly the significance of 1968: 'It was then ... that our eyes and minds opened ... and that we came to the conclusion: our task should be above all the creation of real sentences',[12] and then he went on to enumerate four features which, he thought, distinguished himself and his fellow-poets from other literary formations. According to Barańczak the poets of the New Wave had 'a democratic attitude to the reader', they were committed to 'a dialectical development of thought processes', they had an 'empirical attitude' to reality, and, finally, they were engaged in incessant warfare with the press and the media. In other words, they fought against all kinds of 'false consciousness' and most tenaciously against the deliberately-spread false consciousness of the official organs of thought control.[13]

An important feature of the New Wave was its openness, its farewell to the wonderland of illusions. As Tadeusz Chwin noted in his essay, they held that 'the gesture of negation has to be open' and it was this idea – in the Polish context rather new – which bound them to the ethos of KOR (The Workers' Defence Committee) which came into being in 1976,[14] and in a way anticipated the spirit of Solidarity in 1980. Speaking 'straight', cleansing the language of the hypocrisy of official (and to some extent general) Doublethink, meant that society was being prepared for a change in behaviour and mentality. The rise of Solidarity showed that the greater part of Polish society was ready for such a change.

In Poland we can certainly speak of a coherent movement, although there can be arguments about whether, apart from the Poznań and Cracow poets mentioned above, some poets from Warsaw such as Karasek and Markiewicz do also 'belong' to it. In Hungary, however, there was only one poet to appear in the late 1960s whose work withstands meaningful comparison with the New Wave. I refer to György Petri, born in 1943, in the same year as Ryszard Krynicki (Zagajewski was born in 1945, Kornhauser and Barańczak in 1946). Petri's career is interesting from the publishing point of view: just as his Polish counterparts, he began as a rebellious but still 'publishable' poet: his first collection of verse came out in 1969, the next in 1974, and it was only in the late 1970s that he turned to other channels, namely *samizdat* publishers. (For the sake of comparison: Barańczak published three small books of poetry before his first *samizdat* publication in 1974, *Sztuczne oddychanie* (*Mouth-to-Mouth Resuscitation*). Zagajewski likewise had published two books before his *samizdat* collection *List* (*The Letter*) in 1979.) In other words, there is a parallel between the philosophical and artistic development of people such as Stanisław Barańczak and that of György Petri. Both started out from a Marxist (although Revisionist Marxist) position and it was the year 1968 that changed their orientation to such an extent that by the mid-1970s Barańczak left the PZPR and Petri (who had not joined the Hungarian Socialist Workers' [communist] party in any case) could say at a poetry reading openly that he did not consider himself a Marxist.[15]

When Petri's first book of poetry, *Magyarázatok M. számára* (*Explanations for M.*), was published in 1971 he was already known to the poetry-reading public in Hungary – in 1969 he was introduced by István Vas in the anthology *Költ'k egymás közt* (*Poets Amongst Themselves*). Already Vas stressed (and to some extent tried to justify) a central feature of Petri's poetry which he described as 'pessimism'. This kind of approach to reality would not bother anyone in a normally functioning country, but in post-Stalinist countries still nominally engaged in the construction – or better to say maintenance – of 'existing socialism' it could be regarded as hostile to the existing system. Apart from the fact that in the case of Petri pessimism was an inherent quality, his generation started out with certain hopes about the reformability of the socialist system. He condemned Stalinism bitterly in the excellent 'By an Unknown Poet from Eastern Europe, 1955', a poem ending with the lines:

> I do not forgive anyone.
> Our terrible loneliness
> crackles and flakes
> like the rust on iron rails in the heat of the sun.[16]

Yet, before 1968, Petri still had some hope; when in 1966 he started a course of Hungarian literature and philosophy at Budapest University, he was still close to those Revisionists who tried to reconstruct the ideas of the 'young Marx' while debating the ideas of György Lukács, Antonio Gramsci or Erich Fromm. Apart from this philosophical ferment, there was a serious attempt afoot to reform the economic structure of the Hungarian regime – the so-called New Economic Mechanism, which was launched with much fanfare in 1968, only to screech to a halt two or three years later. And while Hungarians were not directly affected by the suppression of political dissent in Poland in March 1968, the August intervention in Czechoslovakia (the planned economic reforms of which did not substantially differ from those elaborated in Hungary) proved to be a huge shock to the intelligentsia – or rather to those intellectuals who thought that the Soviet repression in Hungary in 1956 belonged firmly to the past, that a peaceful attempt at political and economic reform carried out under the leadership of the local Communist Party had a chance of success. Back in 1956 Adam Ważyk wrote in 'Qui tacent clamant': 'Ostatni mit runął' ('The last myth has collapsed …'),[17] but he belonged to a different generation of ex-communists. So Petri, in a sense, repeats the allusion:

> Ennyi mitológiával a háta mögött
> csalhatósága tudatában
> az ember otthon ül s röhög
> ostoba, régi könyveken …

> (Now that all that mythology's behind you,
> you, conscious of your own fallibility,
> just sit at home and split your sides
> at fatuous old books ...)[18]

The title of this poem is 'Winter 1968' – perhaps to alleviate suspicions that Petri has in mind another, politically more 'sensitive' season.

So, although Petri's first book is already imbued by the spirit of 'lost illusions', and the shock of 1968 is clearly felt in the whole message of the book, he still operates within certain conventions. The radical rhetoric of this collection is one of these; and if we try to define Petri's style in the late 1960s, I think we can agree with his critic Géza Fodor who calls him 'by and large a Romantic'.[19] In this Romanticism a recognition of the antinomy of idea and reality (realisation) plays an important role, and while it has certain connections with Hungarian poetic tradition (for example, Vörösmarty), it also constitutes an attempt to define the disillusioned mode of modern consciousness. In an interview given in 1971, Petri talks about his ambition to combine Holderlin and Beckett in his poems.[20] Without mentioning his own doubts about the success of reconciling these two authors, one has the feeling that Petri was not only too ambitious at the time but that he did not quite recognise the nature of his own capabilities – the fact that he was a better satirist than a 'purely' lyrical poet.

The real change for György Petri happened in the mid-1970s, when, after his second book, *Körülírt zuhanás* (*Circumscribed Fall*, 1974) – which shows a temporary withdrawal into 'private life' and an almost complete lack of hope for a political solution to Hungary's problems – the poet suddenly made the decision to renounce compromise. As Géza Fodor points out,[21] this would not have been possible without the birth of human rights movements all over Central and Eastern Europe (for example KOR stimulated the organisation of the Hungarian democratic opposition) and the establishment of *samizdat* publishing (known in Poland as *drugi obieg*). Apart from courage, Petri also needed a supportive milieu, a group of people to appreciate the artistic consequences of his newly found 'direct speech'. While the Hungarian democratic opposition had a number of intelligent critics and even some prose-writers, the only poet of any significance in its ranks was Petri, whose first *samizdat* collection *Örökhétfő* (*Eternal Monday*, 1981) was a bombshell.

Petri's concern with the language was obvious from his first two collections; critics particularly note the 'downward stylisation' of his vocabulary already in *Circumscribed Fall*. In a poem such as 'Extant Poem by Viturbius Acer', where classical references mingle with modern slang, there are two lines which indicate the disillusionment of the 1968 generation:

> A levegőégbe süti farkát
> mind, aki a jövőt akarta ...
>
> (Now all those who once wanted a future
> jerk themselves off into the sky, into air ...)[22]

This kind of brutal outspokenness was not characteristic of the Polish New Wave. In Poland, after all, there had already been 'turpists', not only Grochowiak, but also Andrzej Bursa, and especially Rafał Wojaczek, who sufficiently vulgarised the somewhat stilted language of their predecessors. Petri, on the other hand, set out to shock both the political and the cultural establishment with his defiant sarcasm, which on occasion even went as far as blasphemy (I have in mind his 'Apocryphal', a travesty of the Immaculate Conception). Still, in *Eternal Monday* the most memorable pieces (apart from some very good poems about death, one of Petri's obsessions) are political in one way or another. The simplest of these is the epigram. Let me quote one which describes the ambiguity of the post-Stalin regimes from the point of view of the sceptical citizen:

> Cipőmre nézek: fűző benne!
> Nem lehet, hogy ez börtön lenne.
>   (Mondogatnivaló)
>
> (I glance down at my shoe and – there's the lace!
> This can't be gaol then, can it, in that case?
>   (To be said over and over again))[23]

Another poem, 'Széljegyzet egy vitához' ('Gloss on a Discussion') begins with a self-critical definition of the apology of the Kádár regime:

Ha seggünkbe nem csizmával rúgtak,
azt tiszteltük volt liberalizmusnak

(When they kicked our arse but not with boots
we honoured that as true 'liberal' treats)[24]

The real change (which actually affected the thinking of the whole
Hungarian democratic opposition after 1968), hinged on the recognition
of the importance of 1956 – namely that Petri's generation simply
could not construct a coherent alternative programme to 'existing
socialism' without embracing the demands and the spirit of the
Hungarian 1956 uprising. And so, in 1980, Petri wrote 'On the 24th
anniversary of the Little October Revolution' (referring to the fact that
both the Russian and the Hungarian revolutions took place in October),
a poem where the language uses colloquial terms to 'deconstruct' the
pompous lies perpetrated by the Kádár regime about 1956. The poem
makes references to various 'uncles', which makes sense to Hungarians, who know that many of the 1956 reformers and revolutionaries
referred to Prime Minister Imre Nagy as 'Uncle Imre'. The other
positive 'uncle' in the first line is István Bibó, probably the greatest
political theorist of modern Hungary. But Petri then carries on
naming the 'bad uncles' – a linguistic twist which surprisingly works
in this poem: namely, the Hungarian Stalinist leaders Rákosi and
Gerő:

Uncle Imre, Uncle Pista and Co.
corrected the world's course just a tiny bit.
They were hanged or locked up.
(Uncles Mátyás and Ernő buggered off
to Moscow ...)[25]

The poem goes on punning its way through several lines, focused on
the term 'calculation' (meaning how many victims of the 1956 uprising
there were). Whether Petri's figures are correct here or not is
immaterial, but the poem ends with the truly defiant lines where direct
speech turns into a provocation of the 'lenient' authorities of the Kádár
regime:

Két számot mondok
56
68
...Összeadhatjátok, kivonhatjátok,
megoszthatjátok, megszorozhatjátok.
Csődöt mondott
aljasságatok számtalan tana.

(I say just two numbers:
56
68.
You can add them, subtract them,
˙divide or multiply.
Your innumerable doctrines, baseness is their basis,
have failed, are bankrupt.)[26]

György Petri never bothered to give a theoretical justification to his poetic practice of 'direct speech'. This, of course, makes him different from both the Poznań and Cracow practitioners of uncompromising discourse. It was only in an interview given in 1991 that he stated: 'For me what was important from the beginning is that you have to name things properly. Political oppression was embodied for me – if we disregard a little police harassment – in the existence of an unbearably euphemistic language in which nothing was called by its proper name.'[27]

My discussion of the New Wave in Poland ended with a reference to the spirit of Solidarity. I think the best way to end the discussion of Petri (which of necessity is confined to the first three collections of this very interesting poet) is by quoting his poem written on the Polish events of 1980 and 1981. At the time, as Petri said it later, members of the Hungarian democratic opposition asked him to write a 'marching song for Solidarity'. This he was unable to do, but he wrote two satires instead, the hilarious but very vulgar 'Andrzej and Wanda', and the excellent 'The Under-Secretary Makes a Statement'. Of the two I prefer the latter, which is a marvellous combination of pseudo-scientific bureaucratic parlance with the ambiguous but threatening language used by some state functionaries at the time, who found Solidarity's demands disturbing. Let me quote the final lines of the poem which (knowing what happened in December 1981) sound ominously accurate, almost prophetic. The beleaguered Polish Under-Secretary states:

We simply cannot
work, there's so much noise. So, housewives,
let us, for the last time, make this appeal
to your sober understanding: either you make
your husbands and babies belt up, or else
we cannot be held responsible
and might be driven to perform such deeds
as you would later on regret yourselves.
The key to the situation is in our hands
and we do not shrink from using it to lock up
whole peoples, if that is what necessity dictates.[28]

Notes

1. Zbigniew Bieńkowski, in A. Czerniawski (ed.), *The Mature Laurel* (Chester Springs, PA: Dufour, 1991), p. 281.
2. Tadeusz Nyczek, *Powiedz tylko słowo* (London: Polonia, 1985), p. 11.
3. Quoted by Bieńkowski, loc.cit., p. 280.
4. Ibid.
5. Ibid., p. 282.
6. Ibid.
7. Stanisław Barańczak, *Dziennik poranny, Wiersze z lat 1967–1971* (Poznań: Wydawnictwo Poznańskie, 1972). p. 59; English translation in *The Mature Laurel*, p. 284.
8. *Pamiętnik Literacki*, Z.2 (1985), p. 158; also quoted in Dariusz Pawelec, *Poezja Stanisława Barańczaka* (Katowice, 1992), p. 41.
9. Barańczak, loc. cit., p. 58.
10. Quoted by Nyczek, op. cit., p. 47; my translation – G.G.
11. Stanisław Barańczak, *Etyka i poetyka* (Paris, 1979), pp. 194–200.
12. Ibid., p. 195.
13. Ibid., p. 197.
14. Tadeusz Chwin, *Literatura i zdrada* (Cracow: Oficyna Literacka, 1993), p. 298.
15. *Beszélgetések Petri Györggyel* (Budapest, 1994), pp. 75 and 121.
16. György Petri, *Night Song of the Personal Shadow*, translated by Clive Wilmer and George Gömöri (Newcastle: Bloodaxe, 1991), pp. 16–17.
17. Adam Ważyk, in Stanisław Barańczak (ed.), *Poeta pamięta* (London: Puls, 1984), p. 79.
18. *Petri György versei* (Budapest, 1991), p. 87, and Petri, *Night Song*, p. 19.
19. Géza Fodor, *Petri György költészete* (Budapest, 1991), p. 35.
20. *Beszélgetések*, p. 10.
21. Fodor, *Petri György költészete*, p. 112.
22. *Petri György versei*, p. 97, and *Night Song*, p. 27.
23. *Petri György összes*, p. 161, and *Night Song*, p. 42.
24. Ibid.; my translation – G.G.

25. Ibid., p. 44.
26. *Petri György összes*, pp. 183–4, and *Night Song*, p. 44.
27. *Beszélgetések*, p. 74.
28. *Night Song*, p. 46.

6 Czesław Miłosz's *Zdobycie władzy*
The Structure of the Polish Dilemma

Todd Patrick Armstrong

Central Europe has been a battleground and target of invasion many times over, situated as it is at the meeting-point of the perennially opposed forces of West and East in their many guises: Catholicism and Orthodoxy, the past empires of Prussia, Austro-Hungary and Russia, capitalism and communism, democracy and totalitarianism, Europe and Asia. Throughout their tumultuous histories and centuries of foreign occupations, the peoples of Central Europe have struggled to retain cultural identities, and accompanying strong literary traditions. It has often been through literature that these nations have been able not only to recall their heritage, preserving it for future generations, but also to understand and interrogate a difficult and often tragic past; indeed, 'the most striking feature in Central European literature is its awareness of history, both as the past and the present.'[1] Poland in this sense is no exception; many works of the nineteenth century, for example – when Poland ceased to exist as a political entity – examine the choices that Poles faced when forced to cast allegiance either to Poland or to a foreign occupier. Such works function as crucibles of self-examination under the enormous pressures of history. This tendency finds an intensification in twentieth-century Polish literature, particularly in those works that attempt to understand that most cataclysmic period of Poland's history, when the land between the Elbe and Vistula rivers, after a brief period of independence, was divided by Hitler and Stalin in the infamous Molotov–Ribbentrop pact of 1939.[2]

The Second World War, with its modern forms of destruction and cruelty, had a major impact on Polish writers of the time; perhaps more than any historical event, it brought into relief the essence of Poland's predicament as a tragic victim – this time to the horrors of the twentieth century. One of the many writers and poets affected and profoundly influenced by wartime experiences, Czesław Miłosz, grapples with this crucial Polish issue.[3] An important theme in much of his early work is related to the general and specific choices Poles were forced to make at this pivotal point in their history. His novel *Zdobycie władzy* (*The Seizure of Power*), written in 1953, in large part focuses on what might be termed the *Polish dilemma.*

A dilemma is by definition a situation in which one must choose between equally unpleasant alternatives. It would be an understatement to describe the many choices imposed on generations of Poles in the course of history as simply 'unpleasant'; this is especially the case in the modern era, for it was during this period of Polish history that Poles were faced with a classic dilemma. The focus of the present study concerns Miłosz's treatment of this quintessentially Polish theme in *The Seizure of Power*, a novel in which his heroes are left with only 'such alternatives as death, isolation, escape, or collaboration with the system – acts that in themselves constitute defeat'.[4] Specifically, I am interested in one of the devices used by Miłosz to analyse and understand the structure of this dilemma: the frame.

By frame I have in mind any element in the text that in some way encloses another element or elements. It can consist of a literal frame, for example the use of a window, door or other concrete frame structure to enclose a moment of action or important image or detail; or it may be a part of the text that forms a figurative frame, as in the use of narrative to enclose other segments of the text. When we consider the structure of the frame, we must focus not only on what is enclosed, but also on what is excluded, and on the frame itself – its composition and location. Miłosz's essay, 'Looking for a Center: On the Poetry of Central Europe', sheds light on the structure of the framing device in *The Seizure of Power.*[5] In his essay, Miłosz writes of the specific geography, of the notions of space in this part of the world. Of relevance here is his concept of 'centre' and 'periphery', and the dynamic between these two loci as one both centripetal and centrifugal. More specifically, Miłosz discusses centres of simultaneous attraction and repulsion – the East and the West – and how Poland, always finding itself on the periphery, is drawn to or repelled from these centres. Miłosz's idea is clearly pertinent in a discussion of the frame structure: while on one hand the frame serves to constrict, to enclose and entrap in a centre, another of its functions is to exclude, to consign to the periphery. In *The Seizure of Power*, Miłosz manipulates the frame device in its various forms and functions in order to illustrate the complex nature of the Polish dilemma: while enclosed and entrapped by a frame of external pressures, at the same time Poles are excluded by centres to which they are drawn (or from which they are repelled), and are thus condemned to the margins, to the periphery, to the edges of shifting empires. These opposing pressures and forces fundamentally affect and hinder the ability to find the right path, to choose an ethical alternative other than one of defeat (if indeed one exists).

Miłosz, by his own admission more poet than writer of prose, constructs his narrative as a series of short, episodic chapters, each concerning one or several set scenes, almost like a screenplay; the many images are similar to the individual frames of a film. The decidedly modern approach of montage functions as a way in which Miłosz attempts to convey the horrors of the time. In *Native Realm: A Search for Self-Definition*, he states as much:

> Again, I must repeat here that this is not a diary; I am not telling what happened to me from day to day or from month to month. To do so I would have to recreate certain hazy states of mind that are still not clear to me. I shall limit myself, therefore, to a few scenes as if I were working with scissors and miles of film footage. The frames I cut should be intelligible to a wider audience, not just fanciers of Expressionism.[6]

Miłosz's use of the frame device at the level of individual scenes and images in *The Seizure of Power* helps set the structural tone of the work; a narrative frame structurally unifies these parts.

Professor Gil's story encloses the primary action of the novel, consisting as it does of three short sections, the first two of which function as prefaces to Parts I and II and the third of which concludes the novel. It also gives a temporal framework for understanding the novel: it is the early 1950s, the dreary present of a former university chair-holder and professor of classics, Gil, who is struggling to survive in the new, post-war order, while somehow retaining his integrity. It is clearly the world of another of Miłosz's prose works, written two years before, *Zniewolony umysł* (*The Captive Mind*), in which he describes the internal intellectual crises experienced under totalitarianism, and the ways in which they can be assuaged or denied, namely with the pill of the 'Murti-Bing', and through the practice of 'ketman'.[7] Briefly, the Murti-Bing pill – taken from Witkiewicz's futuristic decadent novel *Insatiability* – changes a man completely; he becomes 'serene and happy', no longer struggling with problems, which now appear to be 'superficial and unimportant'. Most significantly, the pill affects 'questions pertaining to unsolvable ontological difficulties' (that is, ontological *dilemmas*). Miłosz sees in the Islamic concept of 'ketman' yet another way in which intellectuals are able to confront the contradictions inherent in totalitarian regimes: it is an intellectual strategy whereby one conceals one's true beliefs and strives in every way to deceive one's ideological adversary – and ultimately one's self.[8] Gil has not so far succumbed to these alternatives – as other intellectuals have, we can assume – but is instead in a kind of limbo. He occupies himself with the translation of Thucydides; the blending of Gil's narrative with excerpts from *The Peloponnesian War* creates a sense of timelessness and universality, in that the issues discussed in Gil's translation of Thucydides are those dominating the days immediately following the war (echoing also the temporal setting of the principal narrative – Poland during and immediately after the Second World War):

> Pragnąc usprawiedliwić czyny uważane dotychczas za niegodne, zmieniono zwykły sens słów. Nierozumna śmiałość uchodziła za odważne oddanie sprawie publicznej; ostrożna wstrzemięźliwość, za maskujące się pięknymi pozorami tchórzostwo. Zdrowy rozsądek stał się już tylko objawem zniewieścienia, wielka inteligencja, wielką gnuśnością.
>
> (Words had to change their ordinary meaning and to take that which was now given them. Reckless audacity came to be considered the courage of a loyal ally; prudent hesitation, specious cowardice; moderation was held to be a cloak for unmanliness; ability to see all sides of a question, inaptness to act on any.)[9]

Also significant in this framing narrative is that Gil is well aware of the ambiguity involved in allegiance, in choosing sides. He is a peasant who had pulled himself up by his own bootstraps, despite the difficulties and barriers imposed by the old order, an order which he later represents himself as a university professor – an order ironically defended during the war by his own daughter, Joanna. At the same time, though, he has an inner allegiance to the ideas of the new order, as represented by his neighbour, a young woman to whom the university is now accessible, a dream come true: 'Oto marzenie spełnione: uniwersytety otwarte dla chłopskiej i robotniczej młodzieży' ('His dream was fulfilled: the universities were thrown open to the sons and daughters of the workers and peasants'). In terms of the Polish dilemma, his inner conflict is clear: he is drawn by the ways of the new order, and at the same time forced from its centre – for him the new university – by virtue of his association to the old, pre-war intellectual establishment. Gil's narrative frame encloses another narrative thread, which tells Piotr Kwinto's story. Kwinto, too, is an intellectual, a writer and scholar. Arriving in Poland as the war wanes, as a journalist for a newspaper (the public voice of the new regime, which ironically 'changes the usual sense of words'), Kwinto is caught within the complex frame of the Polish dilemma.

Kwinto enters the scene from the East, with the First Polish Division, a force which is to 'liberate' Poland together with the Red Army. This is ironic, for he has chosen the side of his former captors. The ambiguity and awkwardness of his position is made even clearer when he stops at a country estate on the road to Warsaw. He enters the private library there, and a Polish woman whom he meets eyes him with the contempt once reserved for Germans but now bestowed on Russians and the Poles who accompany the advancing troops. Reading in her eyes the unvoiced thought of 'Bolszewik! Jest, tu, czego zażąda?' ('A real Bolshevik! Here in front of me! What does he want?'),[10] he understands the ramifications of his present choice: he is no longer welcome in his own country. To his request for books, she pointedly retorts that there are no Polish books, nor Russian – only French. Kwinto is a scholar of literature, and he has written a dissertation on French poetry, which makes his position even more ambiguous: he has definite connections not only with the East, but also with the West.[11] Moreover, Kwinto has spent time on opposite sides of the geographical frame that encloses Poland – in Paris (Europe) and beyond the Ural mountains (Asia). Aware of the tension of his position from the very beginning, he is undergoing an inner turmoil similar to that of Gil – the intellectual crisis of faith so clearly charted by Miłosz in *The Captive Mind*. Entrapped within the frame of these external forces, Kwinto at the same time also finds himself on the outside of the frame – on the peripheries of the spheres of East and West, drawn almost irresistibly to both. It seems strange to him that he could be attracted – almost like a moth to the flame – to the East of Stalin, the literal and figurative centre of the Russian empire.[12] It puzzles him, since his own father died at the hands of the Bolsheviks in Poland's first struggles with the embryonic Soviet Union. His journey, first introduced through Miłosz's use of a frame based on geography, becomes a quest for finding his own centre.

Kwinto's narrative forms a textual frame around the story of Warsaw and the failed uprising, which are described in the following chapters. In his introduction to the horror of the city, Miłosz uses a telescopic framing technique, moving from the general to the specific, from the panorama to the detail. First he depicts a broad, open plain on a pale summer day. Birds are migrating, and a small shepherd boy watches them. The details that follow, although described as if they were normal aspects of nature, are actually signs of the devastation caused by the machines and destruction of war: swirling scraps of paper, pigeons with no place to land, burning houses, oily smoke, red glares. Then the guns of war are described, and we hear their sounds; we are brought from cannon to light artillery, from machine-gun fire to single shots, and thus into the framed-in area of Warsaw – on one side under siege by the Nazis, on the other bordered by the Red Army, who will refuse to lend assistance.

Each chapter of the Warsaw story encloses a microcosm of the tragedy and conflict found in the macrocosm of the novel; each scene symbolises the fragmentation of Poland. The main character here is Foka. His nickname, given to him because of his love of the water and swimming ('foka' means 'seal' in English), is contrasted to the barrenness of the Warsaw landscape, and its isolation from the life-giving water of the Vistula. Also of note is the fact that this river forms a border on which the Russians sit, waiting, while the Germans systematically raze the city to the ground. Around Foka is arrayed a host of characters, all physically 'framed' in the few remaining houses of the disintegrating city.

A diverse group, they represent the 'other' Polish army, the soldiers of the 'londyńczycy' ('Londoners') who are playing their last card, underlining for the reader the conflicting ideologies of the two major

Polish armies. The members of this ragtag bunch are a far from harmonious group, representing rather the spectrum of factions in the Polish conflict, that is, the many different alternatives from which each Pole must choose. There is Danek, the leader, previously a regular Army officer; Michał, a member of a militant nationalistic group advocating a Catholic dictatorship; Bertrand, a logical mathematician, who despises Michał, and the latter's fascist tendencies; the teenage girl Magda (in fact Joanna, Professor Gil's daughter); and Captain Osman, a mysterious figure who courts death at every step.

These last two characters are made part of a frame story – a narrative embedded within the larger story of the uprising – that deserves brief mention here. Osman invites Magda to the upper floor of the building they are 'defending'. Once there, he asks that the girl show herself in a literal frame – a gaping hole in the side of the house. The point of this 'game' is to draw the Germans into firing, so that Osman can get a shot at them. He is successful in this instance; we then see a frame of death, when the dead German soldier is pulled from the window-frame of the building opposite. What is striking here is that the victim is mourned not as a German soldier, and hence enemy, but as an unknown man, that is, simply a fellow member of the human race. In this frame story, then, we are shown the universal tragedy of war, and how all are caught within its confines.

These and other participants in the Warsaw Uprising are literally and figuratively framed in by the advancing German soldiers. The frame closes ever tighter, as the area occupied by the Poles becomes smaller and smaller. When, as a last resort, the surviving soldiers of the uprising descend into the dark canals of the Warsaw sewers, the frame image becomes darker and physically ever more constricting, threatening to extinguish all light and hope, which is visible only through the manhole – an obvious, physical frame – above the fleeing defenders of Warsaw; we are made to sense their utter terror when someone whispers: 'Nad nami Niemcy. Czekać kolejki. Przebiegać pod włazem po dwóch. Podaj dalej.' ('There are Germans above us. Wait your turn. Run under the manholes in twos. Pass it on.'[13]) This grim enclosure of death is contrasted with a frame of vitality and freshness found in the last scene in Part I: 'Karafki z wódką między czerwonymi i białymy kwiatkami georginii były pokryte rosą.' ('The small carafes of vodka between the red and white dahlias were dewy and frosted.') In keeping with the narrative frame structure of the novel, we once again return to Piotr Kwinto's dubious world, to a meeting of writers in Lublin, the seat of the new government, presided over by the representatives of the new order, Baruga and Piekelski, a meeting where the word is repeatedly turned on its head. This absurd scene, in which the Polish writers are learning to engage in 'ketman'[14] and where they all ardently applaud the Red Army, effectively closes the framing of Part I: the Germans have pushed in from the West, the Russians from the East. This scene marks a transition to Part II, and also a shift in the dominant frame structure: whereas until this juncture the frame was predominantly one of enclosure and entrapment, in Part II the characters find themselves not only centripetally drawn in by the new regime, but, simultaneously, like an uninvited guest at the writers' sumptuous celebration, centrifugally pushed to the outside by the forces of fate. Miłosz introduces the model for this type of framing device early on in the novel, through the image of a cyclone.[15]

> Co myśleli chłopi, oni, których ziemie gniotły czołgi zbudowane w Zagłębiu Ruhry, którzy znali terror, obławy, wydzierane matkom dzieci o niebieskich oczach i płowych włosach aby w Rzeszy wzmacniały nordycki biologiczny potencjał, którzy wreszcie widzą czołgi zbudowane za Uralem – i wszystko przychodzące z zewnątrz, wyrok, dopust Boży, skrzydło cyklonu, który ma swoje centrum zawsze poza, gdzieś na nieznanych obszarach czy w umysłach nieznanych ludzi.

> (What did the peasants think? Their land had been crushed by tanks built in the Ruhr; they had known terror and manhunts and blue-eyed, fair-haired children taken from their mothers by force so that the Nordic strain might be strengthened in the Reich. Now at last they saw tanks built beyond the Urals. Everything reached them from the outside: a punishment, a calamity, the edge of the cyclone was always somewhere else, somewhere far away in an unknown country or in the minds of unknown people.)

This 'cyclone' is the political, historical and religious one – consisting of all those forces which sweep through Poland and leave in their wake wreckage and ruin, a chaos that then must be sorted out by the Poles themselves, all of whom in some way are influenced by this 'cyclone'. Its origin and centre is always elsewhere – in the Ruhr, beyond the Urals, West or East.[16] The Poles continually find themselves on the periphery of history's cyclone, ever in danger of being consumed by the centre, or hurled outward toward death and oblivion.

Part II opens with a quotation from Thucydides, a passage that creates a vivid parallel to the devastation of Warsaw, describing as it does the terrible massacre of a city's inhabitants. Piotr Kwinto arrives in the capital in the trail of the 'cyclone': when he crosses the river, he is unable to recognise Warsaw's outline, so thoroughly has it been eradicated. His past life, too, just as everyone else's, is in ruins. Now the groups and individuals which had been approaching each other from West and East meet and become to a certain extent part of a single collective again. They are left to sort out the various entanglements and to repair the damage. For them, the war is far from over; there are new powers-that-be, and only one party now, just as in the story told by Thucydides:

> Taki był los, zgotowany przez partię ludową Korkirejczykom którzy schronili się w góry. Ta godna uwagi rewolucja dobiegła końca, przynajmniej gdy chodzi o obecną wojnę.
>
> (In this way the Corcyraeans of the mountain were destroyed by the commons; and so after terrible excesses the party strife came to an end, at least as far as the period of this war is concerned.)

All must make important choices in the new society. The fates of the many different people for the most part represent defeats of one kind or another: some are rounded up and arrested by the new authorities, falling into the traps set by the Wolins and Barugas – Poles who have joined the new regime; others sell out and fall into line, and yet others keep fighting, and are destroyed (for instance, Kord and his partisan group); Michał sells himself to the new rulers, and agrees to protest 'legally', envisaging long years of darkness; Foka is unable to adapt, and merely exists. He realises his estrangement from humanity – his location at its periphery – in a touching scene on the banks of the Vistula: he parts some reeds, which frame an unattainable vision of life: a group of young people are gathered, naked, playing cards and laughing, happy and oblivious of the world around them. Foka almost reaches in from his peripheral isolation to join them in this Edenic centre of life, but cannot. Piotr Kwinto also struggles in Part II, and in his quest for the right decision three characters come to his assistance: his mother, Teresa, and Artym.

All three of these individuals possess the faculty of truth, a sense of ethics, still intact after the war years, and they try to relay their wisdom to Piotr. His mother has an earthly clarity of vision, and tells him, when he tries to justify the communists' actions: 'Co się zaczyna kłamstwem, będzie kłamstwem' ('What begins with a lie will remain as a lie'). She understands the falsity of the word as spoken by these new authorities. His girlfriend Teresa understands the seriousness of his inner dilemma: 'Przyginają nam głowę i każą łykać świństwa. To się mści. Biedny jesteś' ('They push our heads down and make us swallow filth. It has its effects. I'm sorry for you'). After he tries to interpret his dream of Stalin (in which he adores the Soviet dictator as a Christ figure) she explains straightforwardly: 'Ten sen jest ostrzeżenie. ... Grozi ci fascynacja upodleniem' ('The dream was a warning. ... You were in danger of being hypnotised by your own self-abasement'). Kwinto's self-abasement is as though an equivalent of following something other than conscience in his decision. Artym, an old and respected scholar (and perhaps thereby more immune to the advancements of the new order – in comparison with the forever excluded newcomer Gil), continues the thought, as it were: 'Nie, każdy dziś musi dokonywać wyboru. Również wyboru w wyborze' ('No, today everyone must not only make a choice, but a choice within a choice'). The dilemma is presented here as a kind of frame: a choice *within* a choice must be made. In other words, not only must we make a choice, but we must analyse that choice in the light of truth; the words must be given their true meaning, placed in their true frame of reference. In the end, Kwinto decides to leave Poland, exiting from the framework, as it were, and indeed does so – as a foreign correspondent for the new regime. Self-imposed exile, though, is not a victory: by leaving, he abandons what ought to be the true centre for every Pole – Poland. In this light, a key to the Polish dilemma is found in Professor Gil's story. At the very beginning of the novel, as Gil absent-mindedly stares out of the physical frame of the window, his gaze rests on an image that adumbrates and resonates with the many frames that appear throughout the work:

Profesor zaniósł szklankę od herbaty do kuchni, spojrzał przez okno kuchenne w głąb ciemnego podwórza, na dnie którego, między potrzaskanymi płytami, kasztan rozwijał małe wiosenne liście. Tak wiele wiosen upłynęło od tamtej wiosny która przyniosła za sobą koniec wojny, przesiedlania ludności i epidemię tyfusu.

(Professor Gil took his empty glass to the kitchen and looked through the window into the dark courtyard where in the centre, between the broken flagstones, a chestnut showed its first small green leaves. So many springs had come and gone by since the one which had brought the end of the war, the transfer of populations, an epidemic of typhus.)

Framed by the destruction of the war, evinced here by the shattered flagstones, grows a chestnut tree, a harbinger of spring, a symbol of life, of the truth. In the last stages of his search for an alternative (for his exile cannot truly be considered the 'right' decision), Piotr Kwinto twice senses the symbolic centre as represented by trees. The first time he perceives this with Teresa, in another clear instance of framing:

Pnie drzew za oknem były czarne w słonecznym blasku, w ich walce miały w sobie nieporównaną gęstość rzeczy w pełni istniejących. Miejsce, gdzie wyrastały z płaskiej ziemi, było naprawdę miejscem wzrostu, tworzenia się formy.

(The trunks of trees outside the window were black against the glare of the sun and their cylindrical shapes had the incomparable destiny of things in the fullness of existence. The place where they sprang from the flat earth was a place of growth, of genesis, of the creation of form.)

Another example of tree symbolism Kwinto associates with Artym, namely when he sees in the old man a source of comfort and intercession, a centre of humanity in the chaotic frame of wartime Poland:

Jaśniej też widział, dlaczego ciągnęło go do Artyma: szukał przewodnika, mędrca, ktory by mu pomógł w jego wątpliwościach; po prostu, znów jak w dzieciństwie, tęsknił do wielkiego drzewa.

(And he saw more clearly now why he was attracted to Artym: he was looking for a paraclete, a guide to help him when he was assailed by doubts. As in his childhood, he was simply longing for a large tree.)

In these images of the chestnut tree growing amid the wreckage of Poland, with organic strength and silent testimony to the ages, therefore, is the intimation of hope for a Polish centre. It would appear, though, that Kwinto has failed in his quest, for as he rises up into the air, Poland vanishes, 'przysypana na wieki śniegiem' ('covered in snow forever').[17]

In the structure of this work, the narrative has not ended; the novel instead returns to the present of Professor Gil's lonely apartment. Symmetrically closing the general framing structure, this final part opens as Gil finishes translating a line of Greek. His final thoughts turn to a current newspaper, in which he must decode the news – the novel ends, therefore, where it began, with a statement about the treatment of the word, of truth. While there are no overt solutions offered to the many conflicts and dilemmas presented in the novel, we are not, however, left without hope. As the tramcars rattle past (just as they did in the beginning) Gil thinks aloud:

Zamiast zastanawiać się nad tym – lepiej jest stawiać jedynie ważne pytanie: czy umie się być wolnym od smutku i obojętności.

(But was it not better, instead, to ponder the only important question: how a man could preserve himself from the taint of sadness and indifference.)

To be 'free from sadness and indifference' is the same as consciously making and living with a choice – potentially the right choice.[18] It is also paramount to setting down the truth, for the truth is always part of this choice, the 'choice within a choice' ('wybor w wyborze'). In the end, the right choice – the attainment of the final truth – is the true 'seizure of power'.

Notes

1. Czesław Miłosz, 'Central European Attitudes', *Cross Currents 5. A Yearbook of Central European Culture* (1986), p. 101.
2. Miłosz notes that 'the Molotov–Ribbentrop Pact of 1939, which divided territories, has to be regarded as epoch-making' (*Cross Currents 5*, p. 102; see also his chapter 'The Peace Boundary' in Czesław Miłosz, *Native Realm: A Search for Self-Definition*, translated by Catherine S. Leach (Berkeley: University of California Press, 1968), pp. 203–28); in his Nobel Lecture, Miłosz also cites this pact as one of two events that took place in Poland that ought to be forever remembered, 'publicly denounced' and 'confessed' as 'crimes against human rights': Czesław Miłosz, *Beginning With My Streets. Essays and Recollections*, translated by Madeline G. Levine (New York: Farrar, Strauss & Giroux, 1982). The other event

he has in mind is the massacre of Polish officers at Katyń, a crime for which Russia recently took responsibility: see also Jerzy Krzyżanowski's paper, presented at the 1995 V World Congress of the ICCEES in Warsaw: 'The Katyń Theme in World Literature'; Professor Krzyżanowski has also recently published an anthology of Katyń literature: *Katyń w literaturze: międzynarodowa antologia poezji, dramatu i prozy* (Lublin: Norbertinum, 1995).

3. Miłosz and other writers struggled – and continue to struggle – with the ethical dilemma of engaging in art in the face of such horror; while this related issue remains outside the scope of the present study, it is useful to consider Miłosz's thoughts on the subject: 'Those poets who had been formed before the war and who survived the Nazi occupation lived through an ordeal that challenged the very basis of poetic art. Poetry, after all, is embedded in the humanistic tradition and is defenseless in the midst of all-pervading savagery. The act of writing a poem is an act of faith; yet if the screams of the tortured are audible in the poet's room, is not his activity an offense to human suffering? And if the next hour may bring his death and the destruction of his manuscript, should the poet engage in such a pastime? A nearly superhuman effort to answer those questions while juggling with despair is seen in the volumes published in 1944–1945': Czesław Miłosz, *The History of Polish Literature* (Berkeley: University of California Press, 1983), p. 458.) Miłosz's creative effort testifies to the fact that the poet should indeed continue to write; moreover, what he creates provides answers to the questions, and raises a monument to the suffering, so that humankind will not forget those who have perished at the hands of man. Miłosz's Nobel Lecture also offers valuable insight concerning this issue.

4. Stanisław Barańczak, 'Forward' to Czesław Miłosz. *The Seizure of Power*, translated by C. Wieniewska (New York: Farrar, Straus & Giroux, 1982) p. xi.

5. Czesław Miłosz, 'Looking for a Center: On the Poetry of Central Europe', in Miłosz, *Beginning With My Streets*, p. 70.

6. Miłosz, *Native Realm*, p. 203. This characteristic is also elicited by Ewa Czarnecka in her conversation with Miłosz about *The Seizure of Power*; Miłosz comments that 'każdy z nas w dwudziestym wieku jest pod wpływem filmu, więc nie trzeba być autorem scenariusza, żeby zastosować taki chwyt w literaturze. Technika filmowa weszła przecież do literatury' ('in the twentieth century each one of us is under the influence of cinema, hence one does not need to be a screenwriter to use such a device in literature'; my translation – T.P.A.): see Ewa Czarnecka, *Podróżny świata: Rozmowy z Czesławem Miłoszem, Komentarze* (New York: Bicentennial Publishing Corporation, 1983), p. 105).

7. For an extended discussion of Miloszs political prose, including *Zdobcie władzy*, see Madeleine Levine, 'Warnings to the West: Czesław Miłosz's Political Prose of the 1950s', in Edward Możejko (ed.), *Between Anxiety and Hope: The Poetry and Writing of Czesław Miłosz* (Edmonton: University of Alberta Press, 1988), pp. 112–34; see especially pp. 125–31 for a discussion of *Zdobcie władzy*.

8. Czesław Milosz, *The Captive Mind*, translated by Jane Zielonko (New York: Alfred A. Knopf, 1953); see especially chapters I and III. Also of interest for the present study is chapter IV, 'Alpha the Moralist' – Miłosz's analysis and critique of Jerzy Andrzejewski; *The Seizure of Power* can be seen in many ways as a response

to Andrzejewski's well-known work *Popiół i diament* (*Ashes and Diamonds*). Levine also notes this connection: see 'Warnings to the West'.

9. All translations are taken from Miłosz, *The Seizure of Power*, translated by C. Wieniewska (op. cit.). All original quotations are taken from Czesław Miłosz, *Zdobycie władzy* (Paris: Instytut literacki, 1980).

10. The English translation, for the most part excellent, fails to capture the Polish here, which is latently hostile in its syntax.

11. Kwinto undergoes an ethical struggle similar to that of Miłosz (see Note 3 above) in his pursuit of the humanities.

12. In *The Captive Mind,* Miłosz writes: 'For the intellectual, the New Faith is a candle that he circles like a moth. In the end, he throws himself into the flame for the glory of mankind': ibid., p. 6.

13. The manhole represents the frame structure from two perspectives: death and the doomed people running underneath are framed from above, while life and the light above are framed from below. The cinematic quality of these scenes was later exploited by Polish director Andrzej Wajda in his 1957 classic film on the Warsaw Uprising, *Kanał* (*Canal*).

14. See note 7.

15. Miłosz makes reference elsewhere to the 'cyclones of history': see, for example, *Native Realm*, p. 264.

16. Note Miłosz's focus on *geography* in the cited passage. Miłosz points out in other contexts the varyious geographical attempts to define the region in the varying perspectives from the West, where the area is known as 'Eastern Europe', and the East, where Miłosz quotes the jocular but sobering sobriquet coined by the Russian poet Brodsky: 'Western Asia' ('Central European Attitudes', p. 101.)

17. Miłosz, who left Poland in similar circumstances, did not consider his self-exile a victory; for an interesting discussion of the issue of Miłosz's exile, see Harold B. Segel, 'Czesław Miłosz and the Landscape of Exile', *Cross Currents: A Yearbook of Central European Culture*, edited by Ladislav Matejka and B. Stolz (1982), pp. 89–105.

18. For Miłosz's views on 'indifference', see his essay, 'Elegy for N. N', in Czesław Miłosz, *Beginning With My Streets*, pp. 58–62.

7 Nationality in Recent Polish Emigré Drama

Halina Stephan

For contemporary expatriate Polish dramatists the question of how to be a Polish writer abroad has turned into another question: 'As a Pole, how can one be a writer abroad?' The key issue here is finding appropriate literary strategies to accommodate the concept of nationality within the literary persona of the writer and at the same time designing ways of conveying this element within the plays. The two best-known Polish dramatists writing abroad, Sławomir Mrożek and Janusz Głowacki, have been writing primarily for foreign audiences; their works usually began their stage existence in translation. Addressed to foreign audiences, from the beginning their plays functioned differently from dramas written in the well defined sphere of a national culture. The triangle 'author–text–audience', which is clearly drawn on the national stage, in an alien territory is unavoidably viewed through national filters. A foreign author, whether he likes it or not, is regarded as a representative of his native culture and his public persona as perceived abroad inevitably includes nationality. The texts themselves, when they appear in front of a foreign audience, are also scrutinised as expressions of a definite cultural tradition. In effect, an expatriate author is limited in the ways he can manipulate those expectations of the audience: he can either demonstratively incorporate the national element as part of his artistic image and use the category of nationality within his characters; or he can from the beginning strive for universality both in his self-definition and in the design of his plays. The works of Mrożek and Głowacki represent these two contrasting ways in which an expatriate dramatist handles nationality. Mrożek deliberately locates himself outside any national context, avoids ethnicity as an element in the definition of his characters and deliberately strives at universality in the design of his plays. Głowacki, on the other hand, exploits his own 'otherness' and introduces it as an important category in his characters, which are designed with an eye to the current increase of ethnic awareness within American public life.

Mrożek has never been comfortable with the idea of anchoring his own identity or the action of his plays in the Polish context. After his departure from Poland in 1963, and his decision to abandon the grotesque poetics which he had practised in his native country, Mrożek for a long time contemplated ways in which he could bring his own cultural experience to the international stage, but do so as a professional dramatist, whose nationality is only an accident of his birth. In a volume of essays entitled *Brief Letters*, written a few years after he left Poland, Mrożek argued against an obligatory role as representative of a home culture:

> It is equally impossible for me to consider myself only an abstraction – for example a 'world citizen' or a cosmopolite – as it is to limit myself to concreteness, in this case ethnographic and cultural. It would be entirely impossible for me to agree, or still less to strive, to remain a regional exhibit, to parade in a folk costume, to speak only a local dialect, and wave off the rest of the world.[1]

He went still further by using his expatriate status to cultivate the existential condition of 'non-belonging', which he explained in the following way:

> Among the emigrants there are people, for whom it is natural to identify themselves with others. In such a case, the condition of life does not quite fit the psychological disposition. Either such a person practises nostalgia and identifies with his earlier self, or he attempts to identify himself with the local population. ... In emigration one can also find a person who identifies with nothing. Then the condition of life fits one's disposition. Relativity and distance become then his natural element. He does not fall into the non-productive suffering of homesickness or ridiculous – because impossible – identification with the natives. What follows from this typology is that for emigration – like for everything else – one has to have a calling.[2]

Mrożek elsewhere insisted on the productive aspect of existence outside the national context: 'Emigration is not only an existential condition, but it can also be a human disposition. One can be condemned to emigration, but one can also value it and, more or less subconsciously, seek it out as one of the kinds of anti-life.'[3] Indeed, throughout his expatriate existence, Mrożek deliberately cultivated his outsider position and spoke of his 'drive to invent himself anew', which manifested itself in his numerous travels, and also in his frequent changes of residence: from the Italian Riviera, to Paris, to Mexico, and, finally, back to his home town of Cracow, which he had left some thirty-five years earlier.

By interpreting his emigration as a personal choice, conditioned by personality and literary considerations, Mrożek deliberately separated himself form the well-entrenched topos of the émigré writer as a carrier of the national tradition that exists in Polish culture. His insistence on maintaining an essentially 'homeless' state as one best suited to his identity was a provocation addressed to the Polish cultural tradition. It was also a way in which Mrożek attempted to escape entrapment by culture, tradition and politics, entrapment by the controlling political system developed in Poland in the 1950s. Ultimately, emigration acquired for him a metaphysical quality: 'The longing for the Big World, so typical for the periphery, is a model of the longing for transcendence. Joys of the person who broke away from the periphery into the Big World are a model of a mystical joy, the joy of one who managed to cross the cursed and bewitched circle of his particular existence.'[4]

This is not to suggest that Mrożek was entirely uninterested in exploring his nationality as a part of an expatriate dramatist's literary strategy. Some inescapable patterns of handling the issue of nationality within literature which Mrożek confronted abroad were the strategies developed by two Polish writers who preceded him into exile, Czesław Miłosz and Witold Gombrowicz. Both Miłosz and Gombrowicz had defined themselves in the context of the culture which they left behind. For Miłosz, the fundamental element of his poetry was the memory of childhood and youth, of the Lithuanian pastoral which he retained in his poetic consciousness. For Gombrowicz, writing was based on a rebellion against his original cultural circle, against the deadly form that required the writer to fit himself into the national tradition. This rebellion against cultural hierarchies and conventions became a trademark of Gombrowicz's writing and through it he saw a chance of transcending the particular and becoming universal in his prose and drama. Writing as an outsider meant for Gombrowicz maintaining an ironic distance from his own cultural tradition through a conscious manipulation of its stereotypes. When Mrożek in the late 1960s tried to reorientate his writing towards an audience outside Poland, he attempted to explore the literary persona of an expatriate writer as modelled by Gombrowicz. It meant that he would assume the perspective of a newcomer from a younger, inferior culture, who enters the bastion of an old, formalised cultural establishment and brings to it a new vitality, a naturalness, a plebeian dynamism. Adopting this perspective in varying degrees, Mrożek developed the theme of contrast between the Western and the East European mentality – which he originally referred to as a contrast between 'Paris and Trzebinia'[5] – a Western metropolis and a provincial Polish town – first in *Vatzlav* (1970), his first full length expatriate play, and subsequently in *The Ambassador* (1981), *The Tailor* (1966; published 1977), *Contract* (1986), and, in a more hidden way, in *Emigrants* (1974) and *A Summer Day* (1983). Conflicts in these plays involved the differences between the thinking patterns native to Western Europe and those representative of the East European mentality. Those contrasts, however, were broadly cast, without grounding the dramas in concrete circumstances, without spelling out the geographic parameters of the conflicts. In effect, Mrożek produced modern parables applicable to a broad range of situations in which outsiders competed for recognition within the Western world.

This preoccupation with the contrast between the cultural establishment of the West and the more vital, emotional, but self-conscious newcomers from Eastern Europe – the contrast treated ironically, without any recognisable details – had its roots in the model of expatriate writing provided by Gombrowicz. But even though Mrożek found considerable affinity for Gombrowicz's poetics, and for a while identified himself with the image of a newcomer from the peripheral culture modelled on Gombrowicz, he began to realise that 'without Gombrowicz I am poorer, but with Gombrowicz I am not myself'.[6] No longer a 'spiritual father', Gombrowicz eventually became for him only 'a distant and diluted forefather'.[7] Especially after his move to Mexico in 1989, Mrożek freed himself from the obligation to represent a specific culture and settled on the image of a professional writer, rejecting the prestige and responsibility connected with the traditional role of a writer as cultivated in the Polish setting. Mrożek explains his relation to the different cultural circles in which he functioned:

I lived in the East for a long time. I selected my own individual path and I do not belong to any groups, parties, or programmes – I simply earn my living. Of course, for all that one has to pay, everything has its price. I am very far removed from what is known as roots, sources. But I chose this [way of life] consciously, so there is no reason to complain. My personality was formed by Poland, but my profession – by the West. By the way, it is not at all a bad situation – to be able to see both sides. But I have to admit to you that it is very tiring.[8]

'Seeing both sides' meant that Mrożek used characters which could be only vaguely described as originating in the Eastern bloc and representing patterns that contrasted with those predominant in the Western world. Only twice did Mrożek make an attempt to fashion a well-defined concept of nationality on stage. He did so for the first time in the play *On Foot* (1980), where he presents a historical moment in the Polish province where a group of people is caught in the empty time between the end of the Second World War and the beginning of post-war Poland. The Polish play *On Foot* is synchronic in its approach to history, showing the emerging new world among various social groups, but in its panoramic approach it also weaves the concept of national identity through a net of sounds and symbols built into the background of the play, a net that functions here as a matrix of a Polish culture.

More recently, Mrożek turned to Russia, and presented a script of eighty years of Russian cultural history condensed into three acts, which occur respectively in 1910, 1928 and 1990. The Russian play, *Love in the Crimea*, is diachronic in its approach to national identity, showing it in three distinct political stages. At the same time, however, the title contradicts the idea of history and emphasises the permanence of feelings which frees the culture from an entrapment by politics. Despite the seeming historicity, *Love in the Crimea* is not about Russian identity or Russian history, but about the myth of Russia and its fascination. The first act is constructed as a pastiche of Chekhov; the second act presents Chekhovian characters in early Stalinist Russia; and the third act – designed as an epilogue – offers an ahistorical synthesis of various cultural leitmotifs threatened by disintegration, but saved by the myth of love and the aesthetically refined orthodox spirituality. But unlike *On Foot*, *Love in the Crimea* operates not with the popular stereotype of nationality, but only with its reflection in literature and cultural mythology. And if the Polish critic Andrzej Drawicz entitled his comments on Mrożek's play 'How Best Not to Understand Russia', he did so without acknowledging that the play is not about Russia, but about the myth of Russia as it originates with Chekhov and persists in the Western consciousness.[9]

Whereas Mrożek – after some thirty years of expatriate existence – only twice turned to a national cultural tradition as a canvas for a play and the second time focused on Russia rather than Poland, Janusz Głowacki's very successful expatriate plays, *Hunting Cockroaches* (1985) and *Antigone in New York* (1992), have been clearly rooted in the concept of nationality. Głowacki, an émigré since 1981, has from the beginning saved himself the contemplation of the identity of a Polish dramatist in a foreign setting: having analysed the cultural scene which he wanted to enter, he proceeded to respond to the specific interests and needs of the cultural market which he encountered. While Mrożek has always stylised himself as an outsider, even a recluse, Głowacki quickly became a 'New Yorker', an effective participant in the American cultural industry. Within the same image of dramatist as a professional, with which both playwrights identify, nationality occupies a different position. Bound by an identity largely shaped in Poland of the 1950s, Mrożek has not really found a functional way of accommodating the heritage of a country located 'east of the West and west of the East' in his writings. For Mrożek it remains a matrix within his persona which is restrictive and which he tries to overcome. Głowacki, on the other hand, much less cerebral in his attitude to the role of an expatriate playwright, has designed ways to capitalise on his nationality by making it a feature of his two émigré dramas, *Hunting Cockroaches* and *Antigone in New York*.

When he arrived in the United States in 1982, following the introduction of martial law in Poland, Głowacki was determined to survive as a playwright in a foreign setting. He quickly gathered credentials that showed his seriousness in treating the writing of plays as a profession also to be practised outside the home stage. His success story shows how quickly he came to an understanding of the rules shaping cultural life in the market economy. With nothing to lose, Głowacki managed to gain appropriate visibility through contacts and institutional grants. He first participated in the International Writers' Program at the University of Iowa; obtained support from Arthur Miller, who was willing to offer him a recommendation; and connected with John Darnton, a Polish correspondent of *The New York Times*, who found some space for Głowacki to publish his occasional satirical observations in this most prestigious American daily. Not without effect was his contact with Joe Papp, a director who regularly supports Eastern European playwrights. The Guggenheim Foundation and the National Endowment for the Humanities supported his work. But beyond contacts and sponsors, Głowacki worked hard at understanding American theatre culture. Prior to writing his first award-winning play, Głowacki claims to have seen 'something like 48 plays' staged in New York theatres.[10] This led him to capitalise on his own immigrant experience in *Hunting Cockroaches*, which indeed proved to have a winning formula and received the distinction of being one of the best ten plays of 1987 according to *Time, New York Magazine* and *The New York Times*. It was also cited as the Outstanding New Play of 1987 by the American Theatre Critics Association.

Hunting Cockroaches has the rare distinction of being a play revolving around Polish characters that managed to establish itself in American theatre. Głowacki is clearly effective in his treatment of expatriate intelligentsia, generating for its problems sufficient empathy and interest in New York. His characters, a Polish writer suffering from 'writers' block' and a Shakespearean actress with a heavy Polish accent, are trying to find their place in New York and in the process blend the 'Polish nightmares' of the 1970s with 'American nightmares'. In the eyes of the reviewers, the Polish characters seem to be readjusting 'from the Kafkaesque state that they have left behind to the more pragmatic, materialistic mores of middle class Manhattan. To succeed in America, Anka and Jan may have to exchange their hard-won, fabulist view of existence (and art) for the new world's more practical imperatives of self-promotion, pest control and the creation of salable work.'[11] Unlike their Polish predecessors, the obnoxious inhabitants of the basement garret whom we met in Mrożek's *Emigrants*, Głowacki's characters are interested in becoming a part of their new setting. Like their creator, there can be little doubt that the characters will indeed make the necessary corrections in their perspective and eventually adapt, more or less adequately, to 'the American way of life'.

Głowacki surpassed the success of *Cockroaches* with his next play, *Antigone in New York*. Written as a reaction to an American version of 'social order', the play reflected the same feeling for American theatre which Głowacki had shown earlier. *Antigone* was written in response to an invitation to contribute a play for Arena Stage's play-development programme, entitled 'New Voices for a New America' and reflecting the present preoccupation with multiculturalism and the raising of ethnic awareness. Premièred in March 1993, the play somewhat sardonically subscribes to the theme of 'New America' by turning to the multicultural landscape among the New York homeless. Głowacki describes his characters:

> Two heroes of my play [are] a former artist who is a Jew from Russia and a petty hustler from Poland, [who] managed to reach Manhattan. But the move has taken all their energy. They have settled down in Tompkins Square Park on the Lower East Side of Manhattan. It is their final destination. Not quite so, as the police are about to make a sweep through the park. But before that happens, a homeless Puerto Rican woman pays them to bring the body of her man from Potters Field and rebury him in the park. By mistake, they pick a wrong guy. Still, nobody notices and the funeral takes place'.[12]

Within this play, nationality – or, to put it more correctly, ethnicity – serves to individualise the characters by slightly enlarging and humanising the stereotypes of nationalities familiar to the American audience. It is worth noting, however, that Głowacki – while writing a truly well-structured play – manages to capitalise on the American political currents to introduce two nationalities with which he is most familiar: Polish and Russian. With much insight he orchestrates and manoeuvres American ethnic stereotypes and, ironically, by doing so, legitimises both nationalities within the present landscape of the 'politically correct' world.

Written essentially for American audiences, both plays have been successful in European theatres. *Antigone in New York*, in particular, was well received in Eastern Europe and in Russia, indicating that the text, specifically designed for an American audience, retained its validity even when an image of a nationality was presented in front of the home audience.

Since the concept of nationality in recent years has begun to play a more significant role in cultural life, it is obvious that Głowacki's strategy of accommodating it in his plays has proved more effective on stage than Mrożek's distant universality. By comparison with Głowacki's pragmatic strategies of approaching ethnicity on stage,

Mrożek may appear isolated from the present realities of theatrical existence. But in fact, although more resentful of the concept of the Western version of 'social order' than Głowacki, Mrożek submitted the first act of *Love in the Crimea* – written in French – for a competition for the best play by a French playwright and won generous sponsorship for staging the play in the Théâtre de la Colline in Paris in October 1994. The competition was sponsored by 'Crédit Industriel et Commercial', a French banking group – which, it is to be assumed, may have a not entirely altruistic interest in the Russian themes. Still, a commercial undertone alone does not explain Mrożek's sudden turn to the concept of nationality in its Russian version.

Perhaps the final irony of the strategies practised by expatriate Polish playwrights is the fact that they take us back to Mrożek's first story written in emigration, entitled 'Moniza Clavier' and published in the early 1960s. In this story, a Pole abroad acquires a public presence thanks to being mistaken for a Russian because, as the narrator explains, being from the East one needs to be at least a Russian and 'becoming a Russian [gives] me the form which I so needed'.[13] Eventually Mrożek himself, in his *Love in the Crimea*, was to assume the mask of a Russian playwright, an inside commentator on the Chekhovian tradition. Thinking along the same lines, Głowacki in his second expatriate play paired off his Polish vagrant with a Russian Jew. And now, Głowacki as well tells us that he has on his desk his next play, entitled *Three Pretty Sisters*.[14] Alas, it seems that a Polish expatriate playwright is apparently most universal when the Russian Chekhov gives him the form which he so needs.

Notes

1. Sławomir Mrożek, 'Wojna domowa', in his *Małe listy* (Cracow: Wydawnictwo Literackie, 1982), p. 58.
2. Interview with S. Mrożek by Christina Bonilla, *Die Welt*, 6 March 1971; reprinted in *Programmheft der Spielzeit 1975–76* (Linz: Landestheater Linz, 1975), p. 116.
3. Sławomir Mrożek, 'Ich selbst bin ein Nomade', *Blätter des Deutschen Theaters in Göttingen*, No. 449 (1978–79), p. 22.
4. Sławomir Mrożek, 'Prowincja', in his *Małe listy*, p. 16.
5. 'Listy Sławomira Mrożka do Jana Błońskiego', *NaGłos*, 1991, No. 3, p. 164.
6. Sławomir Mrożek, 'Mon cauchemar', in Constantin Jelenski and Dominique de Roux (eds), *L'Herne: Gombrowicz*, No. 14 (1991), p. 377.

7. Sławomir Mrożek, 'Uzupełnienia w sprawie Gombrowicza', *Małe listy*, p. 119.

8. 'Chciałbym przyjechać do Moskwy. M. Zorina rozmawia ze Sławomirem Mrożkiem', *Teatr*, 1989, No. 3, p. 18.

9. Andrzej Drawicz, 'Jak najlepiej nie zrozumieć Rosji', *Dialog*, 1993, No. 12, pp. 116–18.

10. Janusz Głowacki, 'Polish Odyssey: Warsaw to Off Broadway', *The New York Times*, 15 February 1987, Section 2, p. 1. The number '48' simply means 'very many'; Głowacki uses this number in various contexts to indicate excessive amounts.

11. Frank Rich, 'Theater: Emigré Humor in *Hunting Cockroaches*', *The New York Times*, 4 March 1987, Section C, p. 24.

12. Janusz Głowacki, 'Given the Realities, It's Impossible to be Absurd', *The New York Times*, 19 September 1993, Section 2, p. 7.

13. Sławomir Mrożek, 'Moniza Clavier', in his *Wybór opowiadań* (Cracow: Wydawnictwo Literackie, 1984), p. 154.

14. 'News: Sievernich's Irish paradise', *Moving Pictures,* 1 March 1995, p. 2.

8 To Escape From History One Day
Sławomir Mrożek's *On Foot*, *Portrait* and *Love in the Crimea*

Małgorzata Sugiera

The first discussions of Sławomir Mrożek's vision of history began with the publication of *The Tailor*.[1] This play – supposedly written immediately after *Tango* (1964) – appeared in print as late as 1977, and it was generally associated with Witold Gombrowicz's *Operetta*. In spite of numerous similarities between these two plays, their authors' reflections on the history of the twentieth century are very different. In *Operetta*, Gombrowicz identifies nudity with the youth of biology and cosmos, viewing clothes as the epitome of physical and cultural old age, whereas Mrożek contrasts civilisation and barbarism in a decorative way, rather than as the mainspring of the story. Onucy and his barbarians definitely come from outside, independent of the social and political structure of the state of His Excellency. Moreover, in Mrożek's play, the costumes neither stand for nor indicate specific social classes. They cover what is natural, which is only because matter is limited to pure existence, and matter in itself cannot produce meanings. This is where the Tailor's dream ('I will cover everything, and thus will give meaning to everything')[2] comes from. In Mrożek's drama, the opposition of barbarism and civilisation does not mean a diachronic sequence of creative chaos and defunct order as presented in *Operetta*, but a simultaneous opposition of meaningless and meaningful, material fact and abstract symbol, body and soul, biology and ideology. Hence the opposition between the Tailor and Carlos, a young idealist, who joins the barbarians. The Tailor is an idealist in the same way as Carlos, and his idea of fashion strongly resembles the utopian equality of communism, based on dialectics. In *The Tailor*, as in

Mrożek's later play, *Vatzlav* (1968), he points to an alliance between protesting young people and communist ideology (rather obvious at the time). From the perspective of his later dramas, the meeting of the barbarian Onucy and Nana, the Tailor's first client, seems of importance. Their relationship shows, for the first time in his works, that Mrożek has made a clear distinction between what is historic and what is personal. It is only through a meeting of two real people that the terms of living together in 'medium' temperatures – as Gombrowicz would have put it – may be defined out of the degeneration of ideology, dangerous both when it praises naked nature and when it aspires to perfect equality, regardless of biological conditions.

It is noteworthy that Mrożek decided to publish *The Tailor* at a time when his art was undergoing specific changes. In one of the *Małe Listy* (*Brief Letters*), entitled 'Zaniedbana relacja' ('A Neglected Relation'), he wrote: 'I, alone with myself; I and another human being; I and society; I and the metaphysical. Four basic relations, four dimensions of my being.'[3] The theatre of today is interested only in the following three relations: a character and his own psyche, society, or the metaphysics of his partners. The relationship between two human beings, however crucial in theatre throughout time, seems to be overlooked. At about the same time, a certain dualism appeared in Mrożek's plays. There were *The Hunchback*, *Contract* and *The Ambassador*, in which the models of action taken from other authors serve as useful bases for a thorough presentation of the microcosm of human interactions. On the other hand, there were *On Foot* and *Portrait*, in which Mrożek used many obviously unique facts and phenomena, transforming them into obvious model situations and experiences – with historical bases, however.

In *On Foot* (1980), the stage design shows the sky, the horizon and a field. The action takes place in 1945. Somewhere in the vicinity is the front line moving westwards. There are armies, exploding bullets, and planes. The short scenes of the first act, as in a sort of montage of facts, rather than photographs, present the characters in couples, soon to meet at a railway station, who are lost somewhere in an open field. The characters come from different social classes, creating a miniature model of Polish society, even though all of them have individual features, which are manifested most notably in their language. However, this realism gradually fades out. The train they are waiting

for symbolises either the horrors of the recent war and mass deporta-
tions, or a new life about to come. Alcohol and violin music provided
by an enigmatic Musician turn the accidental meeting into a national
psychodrama. In the finale of the second act, the clattering of an
approaching (yet invisible) train is heard. The human detritus is left to
its own destiny, carelessly beached by the high tide of History.

What is *On Foot* about? First, it is a kind of *rite de passage* from
one world to another. Such is the meaning of the end of the war and the
beginning of peacetime for the two main characters, Superiusz and Son.
The former strongly resembles Witkacy's 'real people'; he may even
be a vision of the writer who, on learning of the invasion by Russian
troops in September 1939, committed suicide. Here, through poetic
licence, he is transferred to the time at the end of the war, in order
to mark its place clearly between the past and the future. Superiusz is
the last remnant of the lost epoch of individualism, terrified by the
approaching triumph of mediocrity. He is left only with a theatrical gesture, with which – like Wyspiański's Konrad in *Wyzwolenie*
(*Liberation*) – he ordains the rite of 'contemporary Poland', which has
to be the 'funeral banquet, wedding and baptism'.[4] During the course
of only one night, between wartime and peacetime, we see the real face
of the new world, the birth of which is so eagerly awaited by Son, who
is only fourteen years old. To him, the end of the war means the
beginning of a new life; the historical turning-point has a biological
dimension, and the new, which is about to emerge, is also an unknown,
adult life. The symbolic crossing of the threshold into adult age takes
place during the rite initiated by Superiusz. The 'funeral banquet,
wedding and baptism', constituting the quintessence of normal life,
become a fundamental experience in the approaching world. Human
nature does not change rapidly, after all. Death and the evanescence of
destiny are the truths that every adult person must accept. This is why
Son, childishly repeating 'I don't want, I don't want ...', searches for a
way out in the company of a pregnant girl – a surrogate mother. His
futile protest also signifies the lack of hope for a better world. For
his new journey, whose symbolic meaning is emphasised by his
changing shoes with his father, he will only be left with a simple
principle, namely, 'One must be honest, that is all'. Is this a proper
moral lesson, though? Is it perhaps Son, in the prologue to *Portrait*,
who affectionately speaks to an image of Stalin hanging above the

stage? The epilogue to *On Foot* does not answer these questions. It seems too obvious and grotesque to reveal the reasons why certain Polish people began to co-operate with the new authorities. In fact, Mrożek did not write a play on history, even though the action of *On Foot* is set in reality and there are symbols and obvious references to national iconography, literature and mythology in the play.

On Foot is not merely a metaphorical *rite de passage*. It is also a camouflaged autobiographical play, an effort to reconstruct a basic experience, which turned out to be decisive in the playwright's life. It is no coincidence that Son is as old as Mrożek was at the end of the Second World War and at the beginning of the new political system. The writer also belonged to the generation which, in one of the *Małe listy* – against the principles of the time – he referred to as the 'children of the war', because they were fully aware of what kind of alternative to wartime peace was: 'For us, the beginning of a new historic and objective world coincided with our biological world ... This was why we rushed into the post-war world with so much energy and naiveté.'[5] The maturity and youth of the post-war world also become one in *On Foot*, which allows Mrożek to complement his autobiography with history and vice versa.

However, in *On Foot*, there is also another dimension, namely, a historico-philosophical one. This becomes even clearer when it is compared to *The Tailor*, inasmuch as the Musician in *On Foot* and the Tailor in *The Tailor* function in the same way. The playwright gives both of these characters the role of *meneur de jeu*, namely, the coy organiser of events and the janitor of the 'changing of the guard'. The Musician, like Charon, the guide of the dead, is Superiusz's companion on his final journey, watched by Son. But Son first experiences death earlier, in Act I, when, as if hypnotised, he stares at the blood-stained face of a corpse. Now Mrożek is less concerned about Son – he is, in fact, more interested in his audience. Making Son watch the death of Superiusz, he infuses the situation with the knowledge which he did not possess when he was Son's age – or the knowledge which he did not have at that time – that is to say, the knowledge of the difference between biological and historical time. In *Dzieci wojny* (*Children of the War*), Mrożek saw the failure to identify the relation between biology and history, the result of a lack of awareness of their different order, as the biggest mistake of his generation. 'Nothing in history – for us –

could be the same as before, because nothing in our bodies was the same as before', he explained.[6] This is why, in *On Foot*, Superiusz literally gives way to Son as a potential young barbarian so that the audience can understand, earlier than Son, that history, unlike biology, is not linear, but pushes on in inexorable circles.

The following three dimensions can be found in *On Foot:* the autobiographical, the historical and the historico-philosophical. It is only when this is perceived that one can understand how the author's strategy in this drama differs from that of his earlier works. Previously, Mrożek had constructed relatively clear models of historical and social changes, using such apt symbols as the three-generation family in *Tango,* or the clothes in *The Tailor,* and the transparency and logical precision of the mechanism of the successive stages of change sufficed as the main proof of their genuineness. In *On Foot,* he does this in a different manner, perhaps inspired by the tendencies in European art of the time, which – after destroying old conventions – aimed at finding a new method of communication with the audience and an aesthetic credibility in such basic human experiences as birth, death or pain. Similarly, the truth of the author's biography, written as a biography of his generation, guarantees the accuracy of the historico-philosophical vision in *On Foot.* Additional provisions are made in intertextual and iconographical references, which are familiar enough to balance effectively the artificiality of the action and the characters, simultaneously strengthening the play's ambiguity. *On Foot* is a 'stage confession of the generation's offspring' and a concise lecture on the 'philosophy of history'.

It all seems more complex in *Portrait,* even though relating the story itself is not difficult. First, there is the theatrically attractive prologue: the darkness in which 'I loved you' is heard.[7] Then there is full lighting on the stage. A portrait hanging above. A picture of Joseph Stalin. The actor who delivers the monologue stands with his back to the audience. He wears a coat and has a suitcase in his hand. Who is he? It is only in the next scene that we find the answer: Bartodziej, in love with the portrait of the Leader, betrayed a friend, Anatol, for a 'just cause', a dozen or so years ago. Increasing qualms of conscience slowly materialise in the shape of a ghost, who, the more material he gets, the less eager to torment the culprit he becomes. Even the Psychiatrist cannot help. And then, unexpectedly, it turns out that Anatol's death sentence has been changed to a life sentence, and, thanks to an amnesty, he has been released from prison. The ghost exits silently, and Bartodziej sets out to seek revenge on his true victim. However, Anatol wants to forget the past as soon as possible, and he does not even think of punishing anyone. In order to prove that they are both 'Stalin's children', he ritually calls up the ghost of the Leader and falls down, paralysed. In this way, Bartodziej loses another opportunity for just punishment, so he quickly and discreetly leaves. However, his wife soon makes him look after Anatol.

The story is credible and uncomplicated, even though there are ghosts involved. Mrożek, however, added the 'Uwagi o chronologii' ('Remarks on Chronology'), which definitely turns the whole thing upside-down. In this text, the playwright notes that the prologue precedes Act II chronologically, whereas the scenes which follow the prologue in the play in fact take place at different times. Some of them actually take place two years earlier, and some of them several months later. There is a blank in Act III as well, since the playwright moved one scene (a visit to the Psychiatrist) to Act I. The Russian Formalists discovered long ago that there is a difference between the chronology of events and their artistic order, that is to say, between 'sujet' and 'fabula'. In this case, however, Mrożek seems to have put a non-dramatic plot into an Aristotelian action, with its beginning, middle and ending.

Mrożek aims at differentiating the events: he starts Act I effectively, and he equally effectively closes Act II, but he makes Act III a kind of coda, which sums up and closes the previous two Acts. The action in *Portrait* moves in circles, as the second Act starts in the same time as the first one. It also finishes in the same time, as neither Anatol (the Ghost) nor Anatol (released from prison) wants to satisfy Bartodziej's request for punishment. As a matter of fact, in Mrożek, as in Beckett's *Waiting for Godot*, 'nothing happens twice'. Certainly, nothing happens in the traditional sense of dramatic action. 'Something goes its own way', as Clov in *Endgame* puts it. In *Waiting for Godot*, the 'something' is biological time inexorably leading towards point zero. In *Portrait*, the stage action, filled with events, hides a similar leaking of time, which, against our expectations and efforts, causes irrevocable changes. Disregarding whether information against Anatol is merely a problem of Bartodziej's 'inner life', or perhaps whether he is given a chance of facing his victim, the outcome is similar, namely that the qualms of conscience which he has experienced have lost their intensity, and human hatred smoulders. In both cases, Bartodziej cannot reach his goal, because he keeps doing the same thing, that is to say, he keeps looking for a way out of his 'solitary confinement' by using new ideas. Formerly, communist ideology had played the role of a substitute means of contact with real life. Now, the qualms of conscience play the same role as does an almost Christian belief in the need for punishment for sins. And so, in both the first and the second acts, Anatol is in fact Bartodziej's creation. And Bartodziej uses the ex-convict Anatol, and discards him when he cannot satisfy his demands.

The model of Bartodziej's efforts is repeated twice. Bartodziej, with his *idée fixe*, unsuccessfully tries to make the creation of his imagination, and then the real man, fall into line with his idea. In the finale, we see them together. Bartodziej sits on a small chair next to a wheelchair. Then he stands up, approaches the window and, through binoculars, watches boys playing soccer. The voice of a wandering craftsman, shouting 'I fix pots!', can be heard from the street. This last image is supplemented by a kind of an inscription, in the form of fragments of two poems by Czesław Miłosz, 'Duchdziejów' ('The Spirit of History') and 'Równina' ('The Plain'), which Bartodziej reads aloud. The following two lines are crucial: 'trampling the ruins in nettle and mint/how could I judge human deeds'. In spite of the fact that Mrożek uses reality, like Miłosz, he does not aim to judge certain deeds. *Portrait* shows the omnipresent motif of his works, that is to say, the cost one has to pay for separating ideology from life, and history from everyday routine. Here, however, he adds his own commentary, pointing to the impact of time, which helps life win against the utopian claims of the intellect. Only ideologists think that a cause must have a consequence and vice versa. Such is the meaning of life. Boys play soccer again, and there are new holes in pots – as usual.

In the finale of *Portrait,* it is evident how far Mrożek had moved since *The Tailor*. In that play he believed in History as a concept, a recurring and inevitable model of change, more important than its essence, namely, historicity. In *On Foot*, he found a place where biological and historical times are not concurrent; it was the first time that he acknowledged the truth of individual experience over 'objective' (intellectually proven) knowledge. In *Portrait*, he started to look for the truth of the world in historicity, the unpredictability of life, and also in chaos, which gains meaning from human emotions and everyday interactions. The best proof of the truth of individual experience is found in *Love in the Crimea*, where the playwright judges history, simultaneously showing how to flee from it.

In several of his interviews, Mrożek has admitted that *Love in the Crimea* was intended to be his first epic play. If we consider an epic play to be one in which events do not develop spontaneously but whose sequence and interrelations are rather decided by the playwright (who treats the stage action as an illustration of a thesis), it seems that in this Mrożek is successful. In fact, he has never written realistic plays, but he did construct the starting-point so as to make it all seem that the action – even though openly exemplary – stimulates itself, with no interference from the playwright whatsoever. *Portrait*, where Mrożek stubbornly tried to write in the old manner, shows to what extent he was attached to this traditional poetics of drama. In *Love in the Crimea*, it is obvious that the only reason for the chronology of events and their interrelation is the will of the author, who wants to achieve a certain goal.

The first act takes place in the Crimea in 1910, in the *pension* Nice. The 'love' of the title cannot bloom in full. As in a familiar Chekhovian melodramatic paradox, the feelings are not aimed at those who can return them. The mental discomfort which results from this emotional miscommunication causes theatrical scenes and hysterical gestures. The Merchant Cheltsov reaches for a rifle and shoots. Why? Well, since 'everything continues as usual, but as if ... at an angle',[8] this may be the way in which he tries to keep the traditional order, which, in the play, is marked by the rifle hanging on the wall in Act I, which must go off in the last Act. In the same way as the 'bourgeois' revolution in February 1917 helped that of October, the Merchant Cheltsov's shot brings Lenin on to the stage. And it is he, who in the finale of Act I, will be the companion of the lonely Zachedryński, gormandising candied fruits from a jar.

Chekhov envisaged his world as one in which – to use Cheltsov's words – everything went its usual way, but somehow at an angle. Mrożek, however, does not spare literal allusions; he does not create a mere pastiche. In an interview he says: 'It is not about pastiche. It is not about imitating Chekhov's form. I really wanted to play in unison with

Chekhov.'[9] The playwright only borrowed an outline situation, a certain atmosphere and types of relationships between characters from the Russian master. One of the basic functions of the anachronisms, which are amusing for the audience at the same time, is to point to the fact that we see the past from a present-day perspective. In *Love in the Crimea*, the famous breaking string of *The Cherry Orchard* becomes a specially separated space, different from the one in which the characters move. An exit to the terrace overlooking a vast sea is described in the stage directions to Act I in the following way: 'A framing of a small stage set deep into the stage. The impression that there is a smaller stage deep inside the regular stage is strengthened by framing it with plush curtains, which are now drawn aside and tied with plush girdles with a lambrequin above.' The space of the inner stage – as in theatre within theatre – is supposed to comment on the decisions and actions of the characters, making them an *exemplum*. This is where Lieutenant Seikin notices a motionless ship on the sea, which – for the audience rather than the character – becomes a symbol of the disease slowly devouring the world, namely, the death of the metaphysical. It is not a coincidence that the first person to notice the ship is Seikin, who, in Act II, before a sleeping or hallucinating Zachedryński, will perform two excerpts from Shakespeare's plays. In the finale of Act III, Seikin will appear only in order to escort the longing Zachedryński to Tatiana. Who is Seikin? Inseparable from his horse's skull, he looks like a Grand Guignol Hamlet – a present-day version, that is. Likewise, he is far more aware than the other characters. This is why, in the first Act, he senses or sees the wrong direction history is taking, and he fights suicidally until the bitter end in the army of Wrangel. He is one of Witkacy's 'last real people', another incarnation of Superiusz. Seikin keeps returning to Zachedryński as a remembrance of more sensible times and Zachedryński's long-lost part of 'self', depraved by his compromise with history.

　　The second act of *Love in the Crimea* is easy to understand, because the action of the play develops in a way typical of Mrożek, who feels at home in the year 1928, presenting the same human interrelations as he did in his early dramas, namely, those based on fear and ideological strength. Complex love coarsens now because you need to sleep with those whose power is stronger, searching for their weaknesses in order to satisfy your own needs. Only the two fragments of Shakespeare's plays shown on the stage of the inner theatre prove, in giving meaning to human deeds, that the metaphysical is now replaced by art, which is still not bereft of ethics. However, in Act III, the universal horizon of human deeds sinks even lower. The degradation of the world progresses, as a world without substance becomes a haze of empty theatrical gestures, which no longer constitute any order. The living will meet the dead, who are not entirely sure of their ultra-mundane status; a werewolf in a dress coat walks a goose in a pram, a parody of an Arcadian happiness; Catherine the Great reveals her coronation outfit with the quick gesture of a furtive exhibitionist. In the chaos of mundane, historical and mythical reality, only one direction is saved, namely, America, a shattered vision of contemporary Eden. However, the ship Leviathan – like the train in *On Foot* – will not reach the shore, which is obscured by a thick mist. Out of the fog a forecast of the rule of naked violence and fear emerges. It is terrifying, for Mrożek has given it the grotesque form of a pantomime bayonet hunt for Zachedryński – who crouches, *Angst*-ridden, pretending to be a stone. The chase takes place in full lighting, with a white curtain in the background, which symbolises the mist. The return to the design of Act I, and then Tatiana's apotheosis before the purple-lit stained-glass windows of a Uniate church, seem surreal in the same way as the farcical finale of *Operetta*.

Jorge Lavelli, the French director, who staged *Love in the Crimea* in Théâtre National de la Colline in Paris in October 1994, dressed all the characters in black and white, against the playwright's directions, and instead of a trashy flat model of the Uniate church on the seashore, he showed a Beckett-esque landscape. In this way, he obtained both nostalgia and a tension which grows imperceptibly from the very first scenes of the drama – the tension between the old world filled with meaning and the parody that takes its place; the tension between lost truth and omnipresent delusion. He expressly showed that *Love in the Crimea* is certainly neither a drama about the history of the twentieth century nor a twentieth-century historical drama. The image of the world upside-down, based on the *mundus inversus* paradox, resembles a pamphlet on history written as a drama. The apocalyptic vision of *Love in the Crimea* shows the scandal of history, which gradually degrades social ties and human emotions, depriving the world of reality and turning it into nightmarish theatre. Mrożek selects the place of the action and tells an exemplary story of love depraved by history in such a way that there will be no doubting or questions from the audience. The time of the action cunningly avoids events which were turning points in history. The acts are separated one from another by decades, which both the reader and the viewer may supplement with their precise knowledge of history, or common conceptions or misconceptions, as desired. Viewing *Love in the Crimea* as a pamphlet may explain the problematic age of the characters. The playwright did not want the main characters to age. Why? A pamphleteer appeals to the emotions rather than to reason, and the basic legitimisation of his revelations is the truth of experience, which can never be questioned. Mrożek's characters cannot age, because the power of the theatrical image depends on their century-long experiences, and the vast range of their experiences cannot be verified by the viewers.

The pamphlet works against the scandal of an upside-down world. However, it always opposes the chaos of a world rushing towards an abyss and the relativity of historical events to the unchangeability of the universal values, namely, truth, justice or beauty, which still shine through the filth of the human unrighteousness. And so, if we see it as one basic gesture, it is quite definitely an unequivocal gesture of rejecting history. Using the stage design of Act I in the finale of *Love in the Crimea*, Mrożek makes time return to the point when the fate of the world trembled in the balance only in theory. When he closes the drama with the apotheosis of love (which, in its degenerate form, symbolises a progressive destruction of human interrelations), he adds another value to traditional ones – the complex and simple emotional ties between specific people.

In his autobiography, written at the age of 58, the playwright makes certain plans regarding his departure for Mexico. 'Another change', he wrote, 'I'm expecting – and the impossibility of dreams has turned into waiting for them to come true now – is being able to escape from History some day. I mean History written with the biggest capital possible. The escape from History so far away that it would have the smallest influence possible on my life.'[10] You cannot simplify it all by assuming that moving to another continent is enough, although, strangely, Mrożek's biography matches the changes in his creative works. The successive changes of places of residence, namely Warsaw, Italy, France and Mexico, seem to have been the result of inner changes in the writer, rather than a cause. After all, Mrożek has admitted that the fact that he was born in a country under the power of History was not the only decisive factor in his life. 'The monster kept me imprisoned, but it fascinated me a lot at the same time',[11] he used to say. Well, if this was so, a lot depended on him: that is to say, his change of attitude towards history. *Love in the Crimea* – the pamphlet in dramatic form – is the best evidence that his longed-for escape from History has been successful. For he understands that there are areas which History does not necessarily have to reach.

Translated by Paweł Dopatka

Notes

1. Sławomir Mrożek, *My Autobiography*, in *Mrożek Festival* (Cracow, 1990), p. 35.
2. Sławomir Mrożek, *Krawiec (The Tailor)*, in Sławomir Mrożek, *Amor* (Cracow, 1979), pp. 5–61.
3. Sławomir Mrożek, *Małe listy*, (Cracow, 1982), p. 105.
4. Sławomir Mrożek, *Pieszo (On Foot)*, in Sławomir Mrożek, *Dramaty (Plays)* (Cracow, 1990), pp. 5–28.
5. Sławomir Mrożek, *Małe listy*, p. 186.
6. Ibid.
7. Sławomir Mrożek, *Portret (Portrait.)*, in *Dramaty*, pp. 127–65.
8. Sławomir Mrożek, *Miłość na Krymie (Love in the Crimea)* (Warsaw, 1994).
9. Józef Opalski's conversation with Mrożek, *Teatr*, 1994, No. 4, p. 10.
10. Mrożek. *My Autobiography*, p. 35.
11. Ibid., p. 37.

9 Witold Gombrowicz's Ludic Theatre

Diana A. Kuprel

In his dramatic works, Witold Gombrowicz recovers the basic conception of theatre as a *topos* connecting mimicry (the patterning of play in which 'the subject believes, makes-believe or makes others believe that he is other than himself'[1]) and either *paidia* (free improvisation) or *ludus* (controlled play). He then expands it by appropriating other ludic configurations – in particular, *agōn* (competition) and *ilinx* (vertigo) – as constructive principles. He puts this retrieval to the service of an ontological interrogation, not only of the work of art, but also – and this is my focus – of the human being. That is, his dramatic world can be viewed as a 'play-space' ('Spielraum') or *topos* for the 'mirror-play'[2] in order to stage a particular conception of selfhood as constructed reflexively through form and, intersubjectively, through others. Since the theatre is the very place where human beings can never coincide with themselves because they are always other than themselves and before others, it is the privileged milieu for demonstrating Gombrowicz's particular formulation of the philosophical notion of intersubjectivity[3] – namely, 'międzyludzkość' ('interhumanity').

Interhumanity, by which Gombrowicz understands the forms[4] that become established between people,[5] entails a radical revision and destabilisation of the traditional, metaphysical view of the human being as an original, self-contained unity and its cleavage into a subject for itself and a representation for others. This split underlies Gombrowicz's ubiquitously articulated conception of the human being as enacted and, therefore, discovered in a situation of interaction:[6] the human being is an 'eternal actor, but a natural one', 'always "for another", ... existing – as a form – only through the other', and whose '"I" is marked for him in that interhumanity'.[7] Two points require elaboration. The first is that Gombrowicz's notion of the 'kościół międzyludzki' ('interhuman church')[8] can be understood productively as the collective participation in the fabrication of individuals and social and cultural realities. Paraphrasing Gombrowicz in his preface to *Ślub* (*The Marriage*), the human being, subject to that which is created by another individual, has no god other than that which springs from the other. The second is that, in being formed in-between, the human being is a formal being for whom authentic behaviour is impossible: the external world (other individuals) imposes itself on the internal with the result that intersubjectivity is potentially deformative.[9] Henryk, in *Ślub*, expresses the problem in a soliloquy:

> Choćbym był najzdrowszy ... najrozsądniejszy ...
> Najbardziej zrównoważony
> To przecież inni zmuszali mnie do popełniania
> Czynów okropnych ... zabójczych, a także
> Szalonych, idiotycznych, tak, tak, rozpasanych ...
> [...]
> Ale ci, którzy zmuszali mnie do tego szaleństwa, również byli
>   zdrowi
> I rozsądni
> I zrównoważeni ...
> [...]
> I cóż z tego, że każdy, poszczególnie biorąc, jest całkowicie
>   trzeźwy, rozsądny, zrównoważony, jeżeli wszyscy razem
>   jesteśmy jednym olbrzymim szaleńcem.

> (Even though I was the most healthy ... the most rational
> The most balanced person
> Others forced me to commit
> Atrocious acts, murderous acts,
> Insane, moronic, and yes, licentious acts ...
> [...]
> But those who forced me to commit these insanities were also
>   healthy
> And sensible
> And balanced ...
> [...]
> And what does it matter if taken separately each of us is lucid,

> sensible, balanced, when altogether we are nothing but a
> gigantic madman.)

While Gombrowicz's human beings may direct interhuman relations,
rituals and so forth, in the creation of their particular cosmos, they are
simultaneously imposed upon and directed.[10] Human beings, therefore,
are not only agents striving to determine themselves, others and the
external world, but are also patients, profoundly determined, affected
and victimised by others.

This conception of the human being as subject to a reciprocal action
of goal and limit has a structural correlation with play, understood
ontologically. The insight into the duality of human nature was set forth
by Friedrich Schiller, who defined two drives – the active, determining
'form-drive' ('Formtrieb') and the receptive 'sense-drive' ('sinnliche
Trieb') – which co-operate in the 'play-drive' ('Spieltrieb').[11] Hans-
Georg Gadamer, taking up this insight but freeing play from Schiller's
subjectivity, defines play as a 'governing relation'.[12] Since relation
implies mediation, which is the movement both reconciling oppositions
and becoming part of their unity, play can be viewed as a dynamic
process that takes place between persons playing, person and thing. In
his *Dziennik* (*Diary*), Gombrowicz, defining the artist in terms of
the categories of movement, play and form, states that the artist is
a 'forma w ruchu' ('form in motion'); he is one in whom 'nieustanne
przesunięcia' ('ceaseless shiftings'), identified as 'gra' ('play'), are
being performed.[13] Here, Gombrowicz intimates what Gadamer states:
play denotes a self-renewing, back-and-forth movement and constitutes
a phenomenon with an existence apart from the artist's or
player's consciousness, requiring the corporeality of the artist, player
or artwork as a medium for it to come to presentation. The important
point for my purposes is that what is brought, or comes, into play
and the players are together taken into its rhythm. The result is a self-
dispossession – that is, a relinquishing of autonomy, and a conformity of the self to the game. '[A]ll playing', thus, is simultaneously
'a being-played'.[14]

Gombrowicz's ludic theatre presents the creation and disclosure of
the human subject through alterity. The cleavage of the subject into a
being for-itself and a being for-others is expressed in theatrical terms:
visually, in the donning of masks; verbally, in the at least doubling up

of the dramatic voice; and in terms of performance, in the playing of multiple roles. The human being's dual status as characterised by a 'binding-freedom' under the aegis of play, then, is presented as the ineluctable intersubjective engagement of human beings in the give-and-take, the imposition-and-acceptance, of roles, masks, forms.

For each of Gombrowicz's three completed plays, I focus on a different, but exemplary, manifestation of interhumanity: respectively, the hermeneutic, the dialogic and the semiotic.

Iwona, Księżniczka Burgunda (1935, *Princess Ivona*)[15] opens with the interruption of everyday existence and its replacement by a ludic *topos*: temporally, a national holiday, during which the King and Queen are obliged to 'fraternise' with the common people; spatially, the traditional playground of the park. The temporary levelling or suspension of the established hierarchy is signalled verbally by the chiasmic reversal of the beggar's blessing: 'Niech Bóg Najwyższy błogosławi Najjaśniejszemu Królowi i niech Najjaśniejszy Król błogosławi Najwyższemu Bogu' ('May God the Highest bless Your Royal Majesty and may Your Royal Majesty bless God the Highest'). It brings about a reversal in the dramatic world by opening a breach that permits an outsider, Iwona, to step into the closed world of the court. With her verbal silence, her physical non-responsiveness, her non-playfulness, she subverts the court world, at which point game-playing undergoes a fundamental change from light-hearted fun to deadly seriousness.[16] In order to restore order, the court must assassinate her 'z góry' ('from above') by forcing her to choke on a fish bone at a royal banquet.

The play poses the problem of interhumanity in terms of an interpretation of the self. Iwona functions, first, as an object of interpretation for others, a vessel for their 'obsessive speculation and rumination';[17] second, as a principle of anamnesis and anagnorisis for others; third, as a victim suffering the aggressive acts of others; finally, because she provokes others, as a subject. Concomitantly, the members of the court, who initially function as agents in their attempts to understand Iwona, are transformed into patients.

The passage from agent into patient, and from object into subject, is set up dialogically. However, *ilinx* (vertigo) enters the give-and-take of dialogue, causing it to rebound reflexively back on to the questioning subject. In other words, the question-and-answer structure of the dialogue is initiated by all the characters with the hermeneutic aim of understanding Iwona; then, it changes when the addressee (Iwona) does not function as an actively responsive partner in dialogue, forcing the questioner to assume this role. Once dialogue's separation of the roles of addresser and addressee is internalised, the result is a *perpetuum mobile* of self-consciousness in dialogue form, a 'prawdziwy circulus vitiosus' ('a real vicious circle'), to which everyone is forced to submit. For example, the Prince undergoes a marked transition from using the active to using the passive verbal voice, thereby becoming the receiver of action, rather than being the agent. Having 'caught the cat by the tail' ('Złapałem .... kota za ogon') – that is, having brought to consciousness, and to presentation, the vicious circle which governs Iwona's existence of biological suffering[18] – he, in turn, becomes caught up in and by it and Iwona. His recognition of his existence in the other, that he is not self-contained, is made possible through the other:

> Nie mogę gardzić nią ... jeśli mnie kocha. Nie mogę być tutaj gardzącym, gdy tam, w niej, jestem ukochanym. Ach, ja właściwie cały czas myślałem, że ja jestem tu, sobą, w sobie – a tu naraz paf! Złapała mnie – i znalazłam się w niej jak w potrzasku! (*do Iwony*) Jeśli jestem twoim ukochanym, to nie mogę ciebie nie kochać. Będę musiał ciebie pokochać ... ja ciebie pokocham.

> (I can't scorn her ... if she loves me. I can't be scornful here, if there, in her, I am beloved. Ah, I always thought that I existed here, on my own, in my own way – and suddenly, poof! She caught me – and I found myself in her as in a trap! (*to Iwona*) If I am your beloved, I cannot not love you. I must love you ... I love you.)

The Prince, trapped in a circular polemic with his now split self, literally becomes Iwona's 'obiekt' ('object'), a situation which prevents his being able to act, to kill her.[19]

The attempt to understand Iwona reveals more about the subject than about the object of the interpretation: the authentic inquest rebounds reflexively, becoming, instead, an autopsy (self-seeing). Iwona, functioning as a mirror, reflects the interpreter's own imperfections, flaws and sins, cracking the form, the mask, of royalty. In other words, in confronting Iwona's otherness,[20] the court members find the prejudices and deformities that they have sought to forget or conceal thrown into relief and they come to critical self-consciousness. Iwona's suffering, therefore, has the dual cognitive value of anamnesis and anagnorisis. In Act III, for example, the King has an encounter with

Iwona. As he approaches her, she backs away, fearfully. In reassuring her that he is not an animal, he recalls a past event: the death of the seamstress whom he had raped. In effect, then, the King's encounter with the other is an encounter with the self projected and objectified in the form of Iwona. Through Iwona, he dis-remembers himself – that is, his royal role – by apprehending and reproducing his past in the present, and, in the process of anamnesis, recognising his self once again.[21]

Iwona, consequently, becomes the 'still-point' in the turning, increasingly disarranged and deranged world of the court.[22] The characters gradually lose self-possession as they give themselves over to the game that they had invoked by inviting her into their midst, and over to the power that they themselves have projected on to her. Then they set about to restore their masks – that is, re-dis-remember, re-dis-recognise themselves – by committing the ultimate act of violence on Iwona. The structure of the dramatic action, thus, like Iwona's being, is circular: there is effected a return to the state of affairs prevailing at the beginning. However, *ludus* wreaks vengeance through Iwona. In hermeneutic fashion, the circle is transformed into a vertiginous spiral as the end-state incorporates the new element of Iwona's subjectivity. The court members uneasily and compulsively kneel before her – now even stiller – corpse. Passivity and activity coincide in Iwona's corporeality.

In *Iwona*, Gombrowicz explores interhumanity within the context of a hermeneutic study of the self subjected to the ludic form of *ilinx*. In *Ślub*, Gombrowicz lays bare theatre as a *topos* connecting mimicry and improvisation, and fashions a world of incessant invention arising from the cauldron of pure relatedness to others: here, 'nie ma nic stałego, nic absolutnego, a wszystko w każdej chwili stwarza się ... stwarza się między ludźmi ... stwarza się' ('there is nothing permanent or absolute, but that everything is forever creating itself anew, creating itself between individuals ... creating itself'). Intersubjectivity, here laid bare as the *a priori* element of subjectivity, is manifested in terms of the submission of human beings to the imperative imposition and adoption of roles, masks and poses. Its verbal medium is *dialogue*.

Mikhail Bakhtin's notion of the dialogic or interlocative self, which has an interactive character, is instructive here. Dialogue, Bakhtin writes, is not a means for revealing, for bringing to the surface the already-made character of a person; no, in dialogue a person not only shows himself outwardly, but he becomes for the first time that which he is – and, we repeat, not only for others but for himself as well. To be means to communicate dialogically. When dialogue ends, everything ends.[23]

Thus, according to this view, language is constituted intersubjectively as a social phenomenon and logically precedes subjectivity. Inner self-expression, which takes place through the medium of language, requires this dialogic interaction. Furthermore, dialogue is formative because there is no pre-formed character existing prior to the socio-linguistic operation of engaging in dialogue with the other. Dialogue, therefore, has a creative, formative function since it is only through intersubjectivity that human beings come to be.

The basic question which *Ślub* poses is: 'Is it possible to be when one is alone?' or 'Can one ever shuffle off the interhuman coil?' The play as a whole can be viewed as Henryk's dramatised inner mono-logue: it is a mono-drama in the form of a dream play in which Henryk, a soldier lying wounded on the battlefield in France, returns home to Poland only to find the paternal manor transformed into a tavern, his parents into the keepers, and his fiancée into a slut. Yet, as the opening demonstrates, when, out of a dialogue with himself, he generates his friend and foil, Władzio, and the two then proceed to invoke the other players, it is a world in which he cannot remain alone. This overarching theme is encapsulated in Henryk's monologue in Act III, which, as a screenplay within a screenplay, serves as the play's metatext:[24] alone, Henryk would verify his divinity in a place where he cannot forget that he is not alone, in a place where he is placed before everyone, 'w samym środku, w samym centrum' ('centre stage'), caught 'w obieży spojrzeń, w okręgu widzenia' ('in a grid of glances, a precinct of looks').[25]

The monologue, capitalising on the 'egocentricity'[26] of dramatic discourse, functions as a paradigm of self-interrogation on stage: it is an examination and demonstration of Henryk's subjectivity or, in theatrical terms, a self-conscious performance of the self. Asking after the power of words, after his own power,[27] Henryk 'listens intently to his own voice, examines his own gestures, observes his own mimicry – observes the surface of his own "I", his Form, mask'.[28] Through the emphatic repetition of 'I', he presents himself directly in his role as speaker, thus fulfilling the fundamental condition for the possibility of speech – namely, that someone must say 'I'. By the use of deictic markers ('here' and 'now'), he defines the situation of utterance in terms of his own place in the dramatic world:

Chociaż jestem sam	('Although I'm alone
Sam	Alone
W tej ciszy	Surrounded by [this] silence')

'Powiedzmy to szczerze tutaj, w tym właśnie miejscu, w tej chwili'

('For once, just this once, try to be sincere, in this place, at this moment' [my translation – D.A.K.]).

He lays bare kinesic markers for their subject-defining and intention-stressing functions:

Wyciągam rękę. Ten ruch tak zwykły
Normalny
Codzienny
Staje się ruchem znaczącym, ponieważ do nikogo nie jest
Skierowany ...
W ciszy palcami ruszam, a osoba moja
Sobą rozrasta się na samej sobie.

(I stick out my arm. This common
Normal
Everyday gesture
Swells with importance because it's not intended
For anyone
I wiggle my fingers in the silence, and my self
Swells itself to become itself.)

Self-interrogation is effected by the conversion of monologue into dialogue, that is, by dissolving the defining characteristic of soliloquy – namely, the identity of speaker and listener – into a contrast and interchange between addresser and addressee. Gombrowicz uses a number of dialogic devices in this monologue.[29] For example, Henryk indulges in apostrophes to the following: (1) 'deklamatorzy' ('pontificators'), thereby digressing from the address in progress in order to address another while directing himself as to the appropriate tone; (2) the setting, as when he asks of a piece of furniture, 'Spoglądasz na mnie?'

('You're staring at me, aren't you?'); (3) the spectator, as when he says, 'Ja mogę/ Przybrać siebie w takie postawy ... przed wami/ I dla was!' ('I ... might be moved/ To such poses ... in your presence/ For your benefit!'), and 'Gdy wy wciąż postawy/ Jakieś tam przyjmujecie' ('While you out there/ Persist in your endless posing'). In this way, the purely reflexive quality of soliloquy is suspended. Also, the splitting of the speaker into two or more conflicting subjects is conveyed through the use of particular pronouns (reference to the self in the second person singular). It expresses the split between the rational, philosophical, more reflective side and the self caught up in the 'real' dramatic situation. Finally, he addresses his own speech, such that the dialogic relation is set up between himself and his cry, his 'alas':

> Nie, ja nie istnieję
> Nie jestem żadnym "ja", ach, ach, o bezdźwięczna
> Pusta orkiestra mego 'ach', co z próżni
> Mojej dobywasz się i w próżni toniesz

> (I don't exist
> I haven't any "I", alas, I forge myself
> Outside myself, alas, alas, oh, the hollow
> Empty orchestra of my 'alas', you well up
> And sink back into my emptiness).

Just as role-playing becomes compulsive, so dialogue becomes a compulsion, and as this monologue demonstrates, solitude does not free Henry from its governance:

> Teraz, gdy jesteś sam, zupełnie sam, mógłbyś przynajmniej zawiesić na chwilę twoją nieustanną recytację
> Tę fabrykację słów
> Twoją produkcję gestów'

> (Now that you're alone, all alone, you might at least quit this incessant recitation
> This fabrication of words
> This production of gestures).

Where each moment of the central I–you dialogical relationship indicates the movement of intersubjectivity, here it indicates the movement of intra-subjectivity. Henryk fractures himself and has his self take the place of the other in dialogue.

At the level of performance, this dialogic movement is located in the breach that opens up between character and actor, and the resultant doubling up of the dramatic voice. Henryk is not only soldier, son, prince, tyrant and man-god, according to the demands of the given plot line and other characters, but he also oscillates between various theatrical roles of character, actor, director (as he contemplates various gestures, tones, laughters[30]), even playwright (as he self-consciously controls the conditions for the emission of speech).

By this breach, attention is drawn to the lack of coincidence between the character and the self, to a character engaged in the struggle of self-representation:

> Ja, ja, ja! Ja sam!
> Jeżeli jednak ja, ja, ja sam, to dlaczegóż
> (Użyjmy tego efektu) mnie nie ma?

> (I, I, I! I alone!
> And yet if I, I, I am alone, why
> [Let's try this for effect] am I not?).

However, the struggle is futile: inquiring after his 'I', he must acknowledge that 'Nie, ja nie istnieję/ Nie jestem żadnym „ja"' ('I don't exist/ I haven't any "I"'). The staging of the self is a staging of an absence.

The only way to forge the self is 'outside' the self, in the realm of the interhuman: 'ach, ach, poza mną/ Poza mną ja się tworzę' ('alas, I forge myself/ Outside myself'). The treatment of the monologue as dialogue not only demonstrates the fundamental cleavage of the self into a subject-for-itself and a representation-for-others, but also brings to the fore the latter as the only way of being in this world. To be is to adopt a pre-determined behaviour, to don another's mask and, therefore, never to be oneself. Henryk declares that he has no need for poses, but goes on to adopt poses, discovering that 'Recytuję tylko/ Mą ludzkość' ('I only recite my humanity'). Even when alone, he can only make-believe to himself that he is himself: 'Udajesz siebie samego/ Nawet przed samym sobą' ('you go on/ [...] / Pretending to yourself/ To be yourself'). Mimicry is thus an imposed mode of being in the world: the mask, traditionally used to disguise the conventional self and liberate the true personality, here becomes the self, bestowed by – or donned in response to – the other, as there is no authentic personality to liberate. Role-playing is a malignant, unavoidable, uncontrollable imperative in a world where infinitely reflexive, theatrical posturing provides the only access to reality.

In his last play, *Operetka* (1966, *Operetta*), Gombrowicz reduces his themes to the conceit of the duality of dress and nudity, or form and anti-form, and places interhumanity in a broader context in order to demonstrate that human identity is a product of social and international tensions.

Human identity as the product of interhuman social tensions is shown by the form that mimicry takes as a doubling up, or imitation, which is governed by the symmetry of the duel motif. The duel, a manifestation of *agōn*,[31] comes to fullest realisation in the sexual rivalry of the decadent rakes, Szarm and Firulet. This rivalry assumes the form of a highly stylised and programmatic movement which is rhetorical (verbal flying), physiological (laughter) and formal, and resolves itself into the imitation of one another's words, actions, gestures, costume and accessories. Szarm and Firulet verbally duel with one another until they end up at a real duel, dressed identically. This duel scene, moreover, is repeated except that, instead of shooting one another, they proceed to undress, and thereby turn the duel into an anti-duel. The repetition of verbal and visual gestures creates a ritualised, formalised movement which gives the effect, not of individuals, but of signs duelling. In the process, the rivals become indistinguishable from one another: each functions as a mirror for the other; the back-and-forth duelling motion absorbs the players, changing subtly into the simultaneity of reflection. Identities merge, difference is effaced, shattering any pretence to private, fixed self-identity. Ultimately, the rakes, through their mutual aping, transform and deform themselves into their own travestied self-portrait – namely, clowns – who, in a cretin-like fashion, proceed to chase an ever-elusive butterfly.

The clown figure, representing the ossification of the aristocracy in the post-war period, is, moreover, the sign of nostalgia for a past world that has been irrevocably shattered. It is one mask that human identity assumes as a result of historical forces. Mimicry takes the form of the donning of a multitude of masks which give concrete form to the historical evolution of the twentieth century. At this level, *ilinx* enters mimicry, thereby adding dynamism to the masks and advancing the historical parade by shattering and rearranging the world on a different basis.

The progression of roles and masks can be schematised as follows. Beginning with *la belle époque* circa 1914, the subject is reduced to the conventional operetta role and defines her- or himself according to her or his function within the operetta. In Act II, the political intrigue which prefigures the political revolution takes the form of the sacks of the masquerade ball which cover up the costumes of the future. During the major political upheaval of the Second World War, these sacks are torn aside, and the totalitarian ideologies of Nazi fascism and communism emerge respectively in the bloodied grimaces, uniforms and gas masks of the SS regime, and in the abstraction of human identity indicated in Hufnagiel's naming himself an 'idea'. In Act III, after the horrors of the concentration camp and the extinction of humanity, human identity is reified into a lamp, a table, a Woman.

At the interhuman judgement of the bourgeoisie and fascists, Fior, the master of fashion, demands an end to what has become 'Męcząca maskarado!' ('a painful masquerade'), and that everyone should become human again. In the interhuman vision of the world, 'maska maskę dręczy!' ('one mask is tormenting another'). Fior's summary denounces the tyranny of, and suffering caused by, the deforming mask:

> Przeklinam ludzki strój, przeklinam maskę
> Co nam się w ciało wżera, okrwawiona
> Przeklinam mody, przeklinam kreacje
> Krój pantalonów przeklinam i bluzek
> Zanadto w nas się wgryzł!

> (I curse man's clothing, I curse the masks.
> Those bloodstained masks that eat into our bodies
> I curse the cut of trousers and blouses
> They've eaten too far into our flesh!)

Thus, *Ślub*'s Henryk struggles in vain against the mask imposed by the other and for authenticity – a struggle and desire expressed perfectly by his *Ferdydurke* predecessor, Józio:

> 'Ach, stworzyć formę własną! Przerzucić się na zewnątrz! Wyrazić się! Niech kształt mój rodzi się ze mnie, niech nie będzie zrobiony mi!'

('Ah, to create my own form! To externalise myself! To express myself!
Let my form be born of me, let it not be imposed on me!' [my translation
– D.A.K.])

By the time he gets to *Operetka*, Gombrowicz, has radicalised mimicry
as a fundamental and deforming mode of being. Since the only way to
escape this vicious circle of masks is by the radical act of casting off all
masks, Fior, the consummate demiurge, urges everyone to strip off
their particular form of pain, and conjures up untouchable, holy nudity
– a naked Albertynka. This anti-mask stands as the visual representation of the 1960s decade of love and peace and the celebration of
youth.

Notes

1. Roger Caillois, *Les jeux et les hommes: Le masque et le vertige*, revised edn (Paris:
   Gallimard, 1958), p. 61; my translation.
2. Martin Heidegger's term from 'The Thing', *Poetry, Language, Thought*, translated by Albert Hofstadter (New York: Harper & Row, 1975), p. 179. The term
   expresses not the 'portrayal of a likeness', but rather the temporal 'recoiling' or
   play in the disclosure of entities. Entities are disclosed through their relationality
   with (being-toward) other entities in which they are mirrored; Heidegger
   characterises this relationality as a 'binding freedom'.
3. In the twentieth century, philosophers and literary theorists concerned with the
   investigation and development of phenomenology have inquired into the meaning
   and value of the intersubjectivity of human experience. This investigation led to a
   radical revision of the relation between Self and Other: rather than being conceived
   of as discrete and autonomous, the Self and Other are involved in a reciprocal
   relationship. In this relation of mutual affection, the perceiving, conscious,
   meaning-conferring, form-bestowing Other acts as an essential factor in the
   constitution or transformation of identity *qua* selfhood. As a construct built up
   partly through the instrumentality of other people in the world of intersubjectivity,
   then, selfhood is viewed as arising from a dialectic of being and being-given, of
   choosing and being-chosen.
4. Gombrowicz's notion of form is multivalent: Jerzy Jarzębski, 'Pojęcie „formy" u
   Gombrowicza', in Zdzisław Łapiński (ed.), *Gombrowicz i Krytycy* (Cracow:
   Wydawnictwo Literackie, 1984), pp. 313–46, for example, analyses it in terms of
   the following categories: socio-psychological (form as a value created between
   people and enabling contact); philosophical (interhuman contact depends on mutual
   self-explanation of the personal cosmos); artistic (creation of form); literary
   (literature creates its own form, microcosms governed by its own laws); inten-
   tionality (literary work creates its cosmos in relation to the author – the phase of

creation – or the reader – the phase of concretisation). Tadeusz Kępiński, for his part, in *Witold Gombrowicz: studium portretowe drugie* (Warsaw: Alfa, 1992), takes issue with Jarzębski's broad formulations and provides a schema for systematising Gombrowicz's conception: the genesis of form; the author's self-characterisation as linked with a view of form; the definition of form; the consequences of the functioning of form; the author's reaction to form (see especially pp. 36–67).

5. Form, then, is not limited to the aesthetic realm, but, as a specific mode of human behaviour provoked by interhuman social tensions, enters profoundly into the ontological constitution of the human being through social relations. In *Ferdydurke* (Warsaw: Państwowy Instytut Wydawniczy, 1956), Gombrowicz writes: 'To pewne, że sztuka polega na doskonaleniu formy. Lecz wy – i tu objawia się inny wasz błąd kardynalny – wyobrażacie sobie, że sztuka polega na stwarzaniu dzieł doskonałych pod względem formy; ów niezmierzony i wszechludzki proces stwarzania formy sprowadzacie do produkcji poematów lub symfonii; i nawet nie umieliście nigdy wyczuć należycie oraz wyjaśnić innym, jak olbrzymia jest rola formy w naszym życiu. ... Lecz w Rzeczywistości sprawa przedstawia się, jak następuje: że istota ludzka nie wyraża się w sposób bezpośredni i zgodny ze swoją naturą, ale zawsze w jakiejś określonej formie i że forma owa, ów styl, sposób bycia nie jest tylko z nas, lecz jest nam narzucony z zewnątrz – i oto dlaczego ten sam człowiek może objawiać się na zewnątrz mądrze albo głupio, krwawo lub anielsko, dojrzale albo niedojrzale, zależnie od tego, jaki styl mu się napatoczy i jak uzależniony jest od innych ludzi. I jeśli robaki, owady cały dzień uganiają się za pożywieniem, my bez wytchnienia jesteśmy w pościgu za formą, użeramy się z innymi ludźmi o styl, w sposób bycia nasz, a jadąc tramwajem, jedząc, zabawiając się lub wypoczywając, lub załatwiając interesy – zawsze, bez przerwy szukamy formy i rozkoszujemy się nią lub cierpimy przez nią i przystosowujemy się do niej lub gwałcimy i rozbijamy ją, lub pozwalamy, aby ona nas stwarzała, amen' (p. 87). ('It's true that art consists in the perfection of form. But you – and here we are faced with another of your cardinal errors – you imagine that art consists in the creation of perfectly formed works; you apply this immense and universal process of creating forms to the production of poems or symphonies; yet you haven't ever properly understood or explained to others, just how great the role of form is in our lives. ... But in Reality, the situation is this: a human being does not express himself directly and in conformity with his own nature, but rather always in some defined form and that form, that style, that way of being do not derive solely from us, but are imposed on us from without. And this is why the same man can appear to us on the outside as wise or stupid, bloodthirsty or angelic, mature or immature, depending on the style that lights upon him and how dependent he is on other people. And just as worms and insects chase all day after food, so we relentlessly seek form, struggle with other people for a style, for our own way of being, and, while riding the streetcar, eating, at play or at rest, settling our affairs – we are perpetually in search of form, we delight in it and suffer for it and adapt ourselves to it or we violate or shatter it, or we allow it to create us, amen.' [my translation – D.A.K.].) See also Witold Gombrowicz, *Dziennik: 1957–1961* (Cracow: Wydawnictwo Literackie, 1989) (cited below as *Dziennik 2*), p. 11;

in English, Gombrowicz, *Diary: Volume 2 (1957–1961)*, translated by Lillian Vallee (Evanston, IL: Northwestern University Press, 1989) (cited below as *Diary 2*), p. 6.

6. See the following articles on interaction and play in Gombrowicz's works: Jan Błoński, 'O Gombrowiczu', *Miesięcznik Literacki*, 1973, No. 4, pp. 263–75; Zdzisław Łapiński. 'Ślub w kościele ludzkim: o kategoriach interackcyjncyh u Gombrowicza', *Twórczość*, 1966, No. 9, pp. 93–100; Jerzy Jarzębski, 'Kategoria „gry" w poglądach Gombrowicza', in Łapiński (ed.), *Gombrowicz i Krytycy*, pp. 467–89.

7. Gombrowicz, *Diary 2*, p. 4. In Polish, the fuller passages are as follows: 'ja jestem zawsze „dla innego", obliczony na cudze widzenie, mogący istnieć w sposób określony tylko dla kogoś i przez kogoś, egzystujący – jako forma – poprzez innego. … Przecież mój człowiek jest stwarzany od zewnątrz, czyli z istoty swojej nieautentyczny – będący zawsze nie sobą, gdyż określa go forma, która rodzi się między ludźmi. Jego „ja" jest mu zatem wyznaczone w owej „międzyludzkości". Wieczysty aktor, ale aktor naturalny, ponieważ sztuczność jest mu wrodzona' (*Dziennik 2*, pp. 8–9.) See also Gombrowicz, *Dziennik: 1953–1956* (Cracow: Wydawnictwo Literackie, 1989), p. 60; in English, *Diary: Volume 1 (1953–1956)*. translated by Lillian Vallee (Evanston, IL: Northwestern University Press, 1988) (cited below as *Diary I*), pp. 36–7.

8. 'Earthly church' ('kościół ziemski') appears in Gombrowicz's preface to *Ślub* (p. 91). 'Human church' ('kościół ludzki') appears in Henryk's monologue in Act III of *Ślub* (p. 204). Citations from the Polish text of all three plays are taken from the collection, Witold Gombrowicz' *Dramaty* (Cracow: Wydawnictwo Literackie, 1988). Unless otherwise noted, the English translations of *Ślub* are from Witold Gombrowicz, *The Marriage*, translated by Louis Iribarne (Evanston, IL: Northwestern University Press, 1969).

9. *Ferdydurke* is the best narrative gloss on this process of mutual deformation; see also Gombrowicz's preface to *Ślub* (p. 92).

10. I would agree with Michał Głowiński's assessment in *„Ferdydurke" Witolda Gombrowicza* (Warsaw: Wydawnictwa Szkolne i Pedagogiczne, 1991), that interhumanity and form 'act' and 'function' in Gombrowicz's work by becoming 'constructive principles' (p. 16). In his *Dziennik*, Gombrowicz confirms this observation: 'wszystkie moje utwory pragną być w pewnym sensie (w pewnym – bo to tylko jeden z sensów mojego nonsensu) rewizją stosunku współczesnego człowieka do formy – formy, która nie wynika bezpośrednio z niego, tylko tworzy się 'między' ludźmi' (*Dziennik 1*, p. 28). ('[A]ll of my works desire to be, in a certain sense [certain because this is only one of the senses of my nonsense], a revision of the modern man in relation to form, to form which is not a result of him but which is formed "between" people' [*Diary 1*, p. 16]).

11. Friedrich Schiller, *On the Aesthetic Education of Man in a Series of Letters*, edited and translated by Elizabeth M. Wilkinson and L.A. Willoughby (Oxford: Clarendon Press, 1967: 'the sense-drive wants to be determined, wants to receive its object' while the 'form-drive wants itself to determine, wants to bring forth its object. … The play-drive, therefore, will endeavour so as to receive as if it had itself brought forth, and so to bring forth as the intuitive sense aspires to

receive' (p. 97). He locates the 'bond of union' in the play-drive 'since only the union of reality with form, contingency with necessity, passivity with freedom, makes the concept of human nature complete' (p. 103). There is a conceptual similarity with Heidegger's notion of 'mirror-play' as a 'binding-freedom'. Schiller continues: 'But how can we speak of mere play, when we know that it is precisely play and play alone, which of all man's states and conditions is the one which makes him whole and unfolds both sides of his nature at once?' (p. 105).

12. Hans-Georg Gadamer, 'On the Problem of Self-Understanding', *Philosophical Hermeneutics*, translated by David Linge (Berkeley: University of California Press, 1976), p. 53.

13. Witold Gombrowicz, *Dziennik: 1961–1966* (Cracow: Wydawnictwo Literackie, 1989), p. 73; In English, Witold Gombrowicz, *Diary: Volume 3 (1961–1966)*. translated by Lillian Vallee (Evanston, IL: Northwestern University Press, 1993), p. 57.

14. Hans-Georg Gadamer, *Truth and Method*, translated by Joel Weinsheimer and Donald Marshall, 2nd edn 1975, 1989 (New York: Crossroads, 1990), p. 106.

15. Cited below as *Iwona*. All translations from this play are mine.

16. Here are some points at which the change in the nature of the game is indicated in *Iwona*: Filip assures Iwona's aunts of his sincerity in proposing to Iwona: 'Kpię, Nie, ja nie kpię. Godzina jest zbyt poważna na to' (14) ('Joking? No, I'm not joking. The moment is too serious for joking'). In Act II, he brings to the fore this reversal in his conversation with Innocent, when the latter confesses his love for Iwona: 'Wszystko stało się nagle poważne. Nie wiem, czy pan to zna – te nagłe przejścia od śmiechu do powagi? Jest w tym nawet coś świętego. Jest w tym jakieś objawienie' (p. 36) ('Everything has suddenly become serious. I don't know if you know, those sudden passages from laughter into seriousness? There is even something holy in it. There is some kind of revelation in it'). Later, Filip states: 'Zmieniłem ton, i zaraz wszystko się zmieniło' (p. 58) ('I changed my tone, and suddenly everything changed'). See Gadamer, in *Truth and Method*, on the 'sacred seriousness' of play (p. 102).

17. G.M. Hyde. 'The Word Unheard: "Form" in Modern Polish Drama', *Word & Image*, Vol. 4, Nos 3–4 (1988), p. 725. Hyde considers Iwona as a 'puppet in the hands of the court' who accumulates 'extraordinary and perverse power' (ibid.).

18. The 'kółko' (circle) is at Iwona's instigation (p. 26). The Prince becomes increasingly conscious of the circle. The obsessive repetition of this word promotes understanding: 'Kółko? Kółko? Dlaczego kółko? Jest w tym coś mistycznego. Aaa, zaczynam rozumieć. Rzeczywiście, tu jest jakieś kółko. Na przykład: dlaczego jest ospała? Bo nie jest w humorze. A dlaczego jest nie w humorze? Bo jest ospała. Uważasz, jakie to kółko? Piekło nie kółko' (p. 26) ('Circle? Circle? Why a circle? There's something mystical about it. Aah, I'm beginning to understand. Indeed, here is some kind of circle. For example: why is she lethargic? Because she's out of sorts. And why is she out of sorts? Because she's lethargic. You see what kind of circle it is? It's hell, not a circle').

19. The Prince acknowledges an outside power, in the form of Iwona, to which the court, like puppets, submit and for whom they dance (p. 80). As with the

invocation of the *chochoł* in Wyspiański's *Wesele* (*The Wedding*), it is a power that they themselves have created and over which they have lost control.

20. That is, her biological suffering and lethargy make of her a 'reality principle' in opposition to the court's immaturity, falseness and love of game-playing. The Prince nominates Iwona, 'ty pesymistko, ty – ty realistko' (p. 30) ('You pessimist, you, you, realist').

21. He emphasises to the Queen that he is remembering himself again (p. 51). This stripping of the mask, and consequent breakdown of the royal self, is reflected in the fragmentation of the King's speech and logic: see the progression on pages 48, 51, 55, 64.

22. Hyde, 'The Word Unheard', p. 725. See also the way in which the Queen disarranges her face into a grimace and makes a mess of her hair as she prepares herself to murder Iwona (pp. 71–2), and the way in which the Chamberlain disarranges the furniture in the palace.

23. Mikhail Bakhtin, *Problems of Dostoyevsky's Poetics*, edited and translated by Caryl Emerson (Minneapolis: University of Minnesota Press, 1984), p. 252.

24. As in the full text, in which Gombrowicz, the subject-writer, controls the conditions for the emission of speech, grants to each character a place to speak, and stipulates the manner of speaking the text, so this monologue is complete with sections of monologue and dialogue, as well as *didascalia*. The *didascalia* no longer function strictly as a theatrical subtext, but, rather, because they are spoken by Henryk, are brought into equal prominence with, and thus form part of, the spoken text.

25. Quotations from Henryk's monologue in Act III in English are from Louis Iribarne's re-translation published in Czesław Miłosz (ed.), *Postwar Polish Poetry*, 3rd edn (1965) (Berkeley: University of California Press, 1983), pp. 45–9.

26. Keir Elam, *The Semiotics of Theatre and Drama* (1980) (London and New York: Routledge, 1993), p. 143.

27. '[J]aki jest właściwie zasięg słów?' and 'Jaki jest mój zasięg? ('[W]hat is the real power of words?' and 'What is my own reach?'). The monologue functions metalinguistically in that Henryk reflects philosophically on the use and limits of language. The nature of language as event is radicalised by the actualisation of its performative capacity: language, a form of action, functions, in the intrasubjective exchange between Henryk and his self, as an agent of transformation. In other words, in a play in which the dramatic exchange does not merely refer deictically to dramatic action, but directly constitutes it, in which the proairetic (or action) dynamic of the play is carried by the intersubjective force of discourse, so in this monologue, the real reach of words is that they function, in the intrasubjective exchange between Henryk and his self, as an agent of transformation. Just as the illocutionary force of Władzio's declaration in the previous scene brings about the state of affairs proposed (namely, his self-sacrifice), so here, when words generate realities, effect the transformation, what we are really seeing is the laying bare of the function of *poeisis* (making, poetic composition) in poetic events.

28. Stefan Chwin, 'Gombrowicz i maska', *Maski*, Vol. 2, edited by Maria Janion and St. Rosiek (Gdańsk: Wydawnictwo Morskie, 1986), p. 323 (my translation).

29. For a breakdown of dialogical devices in soliloquies, see Manfred Pfister, *The*

Theory and Analysis of Drama, translated by John Halliday (Cambridge: Cambridge University Press, 1988), pp. 130–31, 136–7, 140.

30. 'Ba, ba mogę/ W obliczu tego podłego, strasznego/ I zawstydzającego świata brew zmarszczyć/ I ręce wznieść do nieba, mogę/ Zamienić dłoń moją w pięść lub ręką/ Przesunąć po mym czole mądrym, zamyślonym/ Ja' (*Ślub*, p. 203) ('Before this vile, inhuman/ Wretched world I might wrinkle my brow/ Lift my arms to heaven, I might/ Roll my hand into a fist or pass my palm/ Across my wise and thoughtful brow/ I').

31. *Agōn* is depicted in the macrostructure as the war between the upper and lower classes, which is formalised as the chorus of lackeys (with their 'Nogi wyrywać' ['Tear their legs out'] refrain) countering the chorus of seigneurs (with their 'Krzesełka lorda Blotton' ['Stools of Lord Blotton'] refrain), and actualised in a corrupted form in the violence and brutality of the revolution. English translations are from Gombrowicz, *Operetta*, translated by Louis Iribarne (London: Calder & Boyers, 1971). A more involved discussion of *Operetka* in terms of the rubrics of play is presented in my article, 'Ludic Form and Formal Ludus: The Play of Masks in Witold Gombrowicz's *Operetta*', *Canadian Slavonic Papers*, Vol. 36, Nos 3–4 (1994), pp. 413–28.

10 The Poetic Messages of Serbian Women Writers in Diaspora

Jelena Milojković-Djurić

In the aftermath of the Second World War, the descent of the Iron Curtain marked the division of humankind into two opposing sides, each of which observed many adverse repercussions of the imposed partition. Serbia, a constituent republic of Yugoslavia, became aligned with the East European Bloc, an alliance shrouded in communist ideology. The political situation in this part of the world to a great extent influenced the ensuing waves of emigration from many countries of Central and Eastern Europe, including Yugoslavia.

The Serbian women writers presented in this chapter – Kosara Gavrilović, Milena Miličić, Milica Miladinović and Ljiljana Vukić – share the personal experience of a divided world. Having spent their formative years in their native country, they brought with them into exile experiences and memories that formed their respective identities. These memories are not always pleasant or nostalgic, but frequently are difficult and tormenting, recalling as they do the many fateful events of their departure from their families and native country.

The selected poems gathered in this chapter present various personal accounts of lives spent yearning for cohesion, trying to bridge the vast distances, both geographic and emotional, that such parting inevitably produced. In spite of the hardship of emigration, they preserved a devotion to their native land, where they spent their childhood under the protective arm of their parents. With the passage of time, their poetic visions became more introspective and memories recurred more vividly. Yet the testimonies offered in these poems were only seldom bitter or accusing. Furthermore, as these poets reached maturity, their mothers acquired an increasingly important place in their recollections. Gavrilović and Miličić became bilingual, writing with great ease in both

English and Serbian, while Miladinović and Vukić continue to write only in Serbian.

Kosara Gavrilović (b. 1924) began to write poetry at a young age, in secondary school, but her early poems are lost. She left Belgrade in April 1941, prior to the German invasion of Yugoslavia. She enrolled in Newnham College at Cambridge, England, specialising in Russian and French languages and literatures. After her graduation in 1945 she taught at the Joint Services Language Courses at the London University School for Slavonic Studies. In 1959 she emigrated to the United States. She lived in Washington, DC, while raising her daughter and pursuing her graduate studies. In 1971 she became a translator for the World Bank, where she remained until her retirement in 1986. She is at present residing in Baltimore. Gavrilović wrote with great perception about her life in the new world.

Her poems and several translations into English of the works of other Serbian poets were published over the years in the *Glasnik srpskog istorijskog društva 'Njegoš'* (*Herald of the Serbian Historical Society 'Njegoš'*).[1] A selection of her poems was included in the book *U tudjem pristaništu* (*In a Foreign Port*).[2] She also published an anthology of her poems, in the English language, under the characteristic title *Walls and Cracks in Walls*.[3] Gavrilović writes her poems and stories both in Serbian and in English.

Gavrilović felt acutely the hardships of cultural alterity in a foreign milieu after her emigration from Yugoslavia. In one poem from the anthology *Walls and Cracks in Walls*, she recounts such an experience. In an unnamed church during a Sunday service, seated not far from the altar, she sees people entering the church and approaching her pew. She moves slightly back as if issuing a silent invitation. Yet all these nameless people nod and smile and move on, leaving her alone. As the church and the pews fill, she feels isolated, as if surrounded by a wall of bricks and stone.[4]

In the course of time, she became aware that the new interlocutors misunderstood her viewpoints, distorting them, or perceiving them in another, different context. In a poem from the anthology *Walls and Cracks in Walls*, she explains her decision not to talk about herself any more:

> We talk not because we want to be heard,
> not because we need to be understood,

but because we don't want to hear the word
of the other and let his word
intrude on our mood and mold our world.

Talk is like the rush of waters through a broken dike.
It lets nothing in from the other side.
Everything is washed away with the tide.

We stop talking only when the other begins to hear us
and having heard, begins to shape us
and build us with the bricks of our own words,
spin us from the wool of our own confusion,
weave us with the thread of our own thought,
tailor us with the blade of our own tongue.[5]

She experienced the burden of emigration most acutely within. She describes with great insight the make-up of a recluse mastering the school of loneliness. Gavrilović singles out the following poem as her portrayal of the inner turmoil that often permeates a life in emigration.[6]

A recluse
is one who cuts loose
the wrecks of his many floundered barks,
each launched in triumph of gifts freely given
and wrecked on the reefs of the other's taking.

A recluse
is one who breaks the bars
of prisons where the other would keep us,
a recluse is the prisoner of his own freedom.

And freedom is a cruel school teaching
the skills of loneliness.
It is an endless trek to nowhere and back, it is reaching
to where one kills and dies, and resurrects at will,
and moves hills,
and makes the waters rise
and time stand still
beneath the falling stars.

The price of loneliness and isolation was truly very high for the poet. In another poem from the same collection, she expresses her newly gained appreciation of the presence of the other in her life. She understands that seclusion meant in fact the exclusion of fellow human beings and the deprivation of essential and vital connections with the community of men and women at large. Only the right gesture of the other could disperse the self-imposed exile within.[7]

In time, she eventually came to the conclusion that she was looking from a vantage point in time at a life that probably never was the way she remembered it. She also blamed herself as well as others for carelessness in relationships that might have caused unnecessary pain. She thought of the words of Oscar Wilde and his exegesis on the human predicament and the unmitigated killing of the souls of the people close to us: 'Yet each man kills the thing he loves ...'.[8] Moreover, she concluded that '... all those who willingly and consciously uproot themselves from the environment in which they were born and to which they belong, must necessarily kill parts of themselves. Some of these parts are so essential to their existence that their entire being is essentially changed, so that one may argue that the original being was killed and a new one created.'[9] She expresses this notion through a series of powerful images of her homeland in the poem 'A Fragment':

> We who have abandoned our country, and our hearths,
> and our gardens, and vineyards, and orchards,
> we who have left behind everything we ever possessed
> so that we may forever remain what we have ever been,
> or what we thought we were, but were not...
> We who have thrown away all our hopes and dreams
> and have renounced the right to our tomorrow ...
> We fugitives, we traitors, we killers of souls.
>
> We who have left behind the barking of our dogs,
> the sunsets over the Sava reflected in our windows,
> the golden domes of our churches, the icons of Christ the Savior,
> and the nights that settle softly over the Topchider dew...
> We who exist outside the present,
> who fly with the Dutchman and wander with the Jew,
> we fugitives, we traitors, we killers of souls.[10]

Milena Miličić (b. 1935) was born in Belgrade. Early in her youth she lost her mother, who died of tuberculosis as a consequence of hunger and deprivations during the years of the Second World War. Subsequently, Miličić's further education was interrupted and she emigrated to the United States in 1956. She married and settled in Bellingham, Washington state, where she worked as an office clerk and a claims auditor in an insurance company. She started writing poetry in the late 1960s using both the Serbian and the English languages.

She maintained a profound interest in literature, singling out Russian literature as the major influence in her writing. A lifelong admirer of Tolstoy's works, she also read the poetry of Pushkin, Esenin and Tsvetaeva. She was a member of the local Great Books Club for many years. Her interest in Russian culture led her to help establish a sister city association between Bellingham and Nakhodka in Siberia. In this capacity she travelled to Russia in 1988. This trip gave her new insight into the splendour of Russia's past, as preserved in the museums and churches of Moscow and St. Petersburg.

A selection of Miličić's poems was included in the anthology *U tudjem pristaništu* (*In a Foreign Port*).[11] In 1990 she privately published a bilingual collection of her poems, *Pesme – Poems*.[12] The poems in this collection deal with the personal life of the poet and celebrates her relations with her family. Her recollections of the past often accompany her visions of the present. She extols the pleasures that life gives us, with its intimate encounters, and celebrates her devotion to her family. While depicting her ever-changing relationship with life's experiences, she feels as one with the sights and sounds of nature. At the same time, she is not spared from tormenting experiences and from the darkness within. There is a an unsettling counterpoint in her thoughts, which casts doubts on the validity of religious canons, while eschewing the loss of faith.

In the early 1990s Miličić wrote several poems reminiscing about her childhood during the difficult years of the Second World War. She felt that the time had come to record those memories that had left an indelible mark on her body and soul. In a message to the author of these lines Miličić wrote: 'Perhaps when one is young, the memories are pushed away. But with the passage of time they resurface at times in a powerful manner.' Such is her recollection of the bombardment during the war :

> 'What Do I Remember of War'
>
> I remember I used to cry a lot;
> at night I would close my eyes
> and pretend I am asleep,
> giving my mother chance to rest.

I remember how hungry I was
many times,
but I couldn't eat
because I had hard stomach pain
when I heard airplanes approaching.
I remember my mothers' pale face,
her eyes tearful, almost sunken in her bony face.
I heard bombs at night
dashing through the air,
fiery vessels,
with all their might ...
I remember when my parents
prayed,
as we do it today;
how insulting it is
to think
that we came here
with sense of purpose.
I remember Jewish people
in our neighborhood
being forced to wear
the Star of David on their hoods.
But most of all
I remember the time
when I was told
that God was good.[13]

She deeply felt the loss of her mother. In her retrospective poem 'Mother's Death,' she records how her life changed after her mother's death, as if the radiance of a rainbow vanished for ever:

Yesterday a Palm was slain
and my rainbow vanished
never having a chance to see
the unbearable beauty of falling water.

My mother was born in heaven
the grass had to grow many times over
before she found her cross.

There was the star roving through the woods
trying to catch the first day of spring
Yet the time was late ...
The sun sprung before the dawn was born
and when she kissed it
she heard a voice from yonder.[14]

There are echoes of the long and difficult life's journey in the poem 'Silent passage.'

> Don't try to translate the
> Silence of my face.
> My journey was long,
> In the process of moving
> I lost a wing.
> You danced a macabre dance
> At a corner
> Where I left my toys
> To someone else
> To play with.
> To love
> And to be loved
> In turn
> Is a blessing
> That gives new charm
> To our existence.
> I do not want anything
> Absolutely,
> Nor absolute.
> When I look at you
> I see a resemblance
> Of what once
> Used to be.
> A memory of the past
> And additional charm
> Of innocence.
> We cry together,
> Separately,
> I always see you
> Farther away.
> I feel desperate,
> For I can't catch up
> With you.
> Yet, you are standing.[15]

Milica Miladinović (b. 1928) is a diligent and outspoken writer. She studied the English language and literature at the University of Belgrade. In 1953 she received a scholarship and studied for two semesters at the University of Nottingham in England. After the death of her parents in 1957, she emigrated to Rome, Italy. As a struggling refugee, she started writing poems, many of which often served as a commentary on the injustices and political evils that permeated the lives of the Serbian population under communist rule. In 1986 she left Italy and subsequently emigrated to the United States where she now resides with her husband in Fallbrook, California.

She has published two books of poetry and a collection of fables.[16] Miladinović aspired to serve as an educator at large and a voice of reason. Therefore, she chose to write fables – stressing the educational value of this literary genre. In the preface to her collection of fables she explains her fascination with this genre early on in her youth, singling out the writer Dositej Obradović as one of her major literary influences. Obradović advanced education and ushered the spirit of Enlightenment in the Serbian literary scene towards the end of the eighteenth century. He saw the great need for didactic literature – the fable being one of the possible tools for this educational mission.

Miladinović obviously cares about children and education. The poem 'Krće' is a case in point. She wrote this poem after reading a report in a Belgrade newspaper about a neglected school in the village of Krće. It should be noted that the first Serbian archbishop, Sava, was born in that region. Sava (1169–1235) was of royal descent, a member of the Nemanjić dynasty, yet he renounced his noble position and became a monk. A man of letters and an ardent supporter of education, Sava became the patron saint of Serbian schoolchildren. That is why Miladinović reacted with concern when reading that in the very heart of this historic region so little attention and so few resources were given to education. The poem 'Krće: Zapis o jednom srpskom selu' ('Krće: A Note about a Serbian Village') speaks clearly of this concern:

> Izgleda kao da je na kraju sveta,
> Reklo bi se da nikome ne smeta
> po svom zlohudom postojanju,
> po bedi, gladi, pustoši, očajanju,
> onih koji niti prose, niti traže,
> onih, za koje se niko ne zalaže,
> jer ponosni nemo ćute,
> gledajući poderane skute.
> Krće. To je jedno srpsko selo,
> koje nije ni čisto ni belo,
> vec sumorno, tužno,
> zaostalo, zapušteno, ružno,
> koje nema ni crkvu ni zvona
> da zajeca bono,
> da podseti da tu ima tića
> porekla Nemanjića.

Ta deca bistre glave,
iz kojih svetle nevine oči plave
sinovi su Svetog Save.
No oni ne znaju za njega,
jer su ta deca lišena svega,
odvojena sa stotinu brega
od nasušnih potreba
i željni suva hleba.
Ti djaci ne znaju ni za školsko zvono
da veselo ih bar pozove ono
u tesne, trule i dotrajale klupe,
da se tu šćućureno skupe
u mračnoj učionici škole stare,
slamne krovinjare,
za koju je i sunce tudje,
jer ne može tamo da udje,
pa daje prednost vlazi i mraku
mesto svome svetlosnom zraku.
Tu deca Krća uče da slova sriču ...

(It seemed as if this village was at the end of the world.
One would think that it would not be in the way of anyone
due to its miserable situation,
the poverty, hunger, devastation, despair
of those who do not beg, or ask
of those who nobody protects
since the proud ones are silently
aware of their tattered clothing.
Krće is a Serbian village
not white and clean
but somber and sad
backward, neglected, ugly
without a church, or bell
to toll a painful
reminder that there are fledgling birds
of the Nemanjić's noble heritage.
These children with fine minds
with bright blue eyes
are the sons of Saint Sava.
They have not heard of him,
since they are deprived of everything,
separated by hundreds of hills
from daily necessities
even of dried bread alone.
These pupils do not know
the sound of the school bell
to invite them cheerfully

into the old worn out benches
to congregate murmuring together
in the dark classroom of the old school
a cottage with thatched roof
too dark even for the sun
to illuminate it,
thus humidity and darkness
instead of bright light –
that is where the children of Krće have to learn
their alphabet.)[17]

An introspective and pensive mood permeates the first verse of Miladinović's poem 'Kada duša ćuti'('When the Soul is Silent'), while the concluding verse projects optimism and positive self-reliance:

Kad je naš život tako jadno kratak
u odnosu na večnost jedva jedan dan,
i bez iskre nade na njegov povratak,
kad svaku stvar čeka crn, večiti san:
Zašto dušo moja tako smerno ćutiš?
Zašto tražiš tamu i kad sunce sija?
Zašto uvek samo najgore slutiš
i zašto ti tuga iznad svega prija?
(...)
Ja ne želim tvoju zatočenost više.
Uzdigni se smelo u svetlije sfere:
tamo gde još punim plućima se diše,
gde trijumf ideja ne zna za stegu, mere ...

(Since our life is so regrettably short,
in comparison with eternity hardly a day long
without any hope for its return
where every creature waits for its final dream:
Why is my soul so meekly quiet?
Why is there yearning for shadow in the midst of sunlight?
Why the worst foreboding
and sorrowful thoughts?
(...)
I do not want the enslavement of my spirit any more
Instead a sweeping rise to the brighter sphere;
Where one can freely breathe
And where triumphant ideas are not measured and suppressed.)[18]

At one point she voices her acceptance of all that life has brought on. She repeats the archetypal metaphor of predestined fate and the inevitability of events of major import. Miladinović speaks also about the memory that lingers on and even becomes more obtrusive as the years go by, as in the poem 'Nostalgija' ('Nostalgia):[19]

Nije bilo teško iz zemlje izaći
kad čovek zna zašto živi, bori se i mre,
kad je grejan nadom da će cilj postići,
svejedno da li kasnije il' pre.

Al' od toga je bilo nešto mnogo teže
I čega smo bili svesni isto tako:
duhovne korene što u nama razvi mreže
rodna gruda, ničim se ne mogu isčupati lako.. .

Jer sreća je jedna, ona se ne deli
I ostaje tamo gde korene pusti,
ona leži tamo gde šljivaci beli
prostru oko sebe cvetni ćilim gusti.

Zato k'o na krstu razapeti mi smo:
izbeglištvo nužno za nas je Golgota,
al' se tebe mila zemljo mi odrekli nismo,
jer ti si sva vrednost naša, smisao života.

(It was not difficult to leave the country
when life's goals were determined
hoping that the projected destination
would be reached earlier or later.

It was much more difficult,
although we were aware even then,
to pull out the spiritual roots that the native soil
has instilled in us ...

Happiness cannot be divided;
it remains where the roots were established
in the white plum orchards
covered with skirts of blossoms.

Therefore we seemed as if crucified:
the necessity of emigration presented our Golgotha,
yet we have not forsaken our beloved country
since it gave meaning and value to our lives.)[20]

Ljiljana Vukić (b. 1940), born Banjanin, completed her studies at the Higher Pedagogical School in Belgrade, specialising in English language and literature. In 1970 she emigrated with her husband to Germany where she became one of the founders of the Serbo-Croatian supplemental education for Yugoslav children in the Offenbach school district. As a devoted teacher, she shows great interest in the life of children and also writes poems describing childhood episodes with a didactic note. She serves as the technical editor of the children's periodical *Mladost* (*Youth*) and also of the Yugoslav Literary Workshop in Frankfurt-am-Main.[21] She resides at present in Offenbach, Germany.

The poetry from her early youth reflects her vision of the world of dreams intertwined with the realities of everyday living. The majority of her poems deal with introspective musing and recollections of special moments of closeness with loved ones. Her love of nature imbues her poems with bucolic and lyrical overtones. The separation from the family at large is portrayed in several of her poems. She also writes poems for children and has recently completed a collection entitled *Pupoljak na dlanu* (*A Bud in the Palm of my Hand*).[22]

Several poems in her last collection *Strela Predaka* (*Ancestral Arrow*) reflect the recent schism in Yugoslav society. She deplores the prevalence of hatred that perpetuates hostility. In the poem 'Nemoćne snage'('Powerless Strength') she compares the pernicious transmissions of combative spirit to an ancestral arrow wounding the young. Thus, she offers a perceptive analysis of the existing experiences as both life-giving and life-threatening.[23]

> Ranila te strela predaka
> u utrobi detinjstva
> besom divljeg konja
> što proplanke
> zorom obilazi
> i svojom kopitom
> obale zemlje ore.
>
> U vulkan nemoći svoje
> izgaraš vetrom snage
> i ljubav žednu
> u ušća pesme
> pretvaraš.
>
> (The ancestral arrow
> wounded your childhood bowels
> with the furor of a wild horse
> tilling with its hoofs
> the shores of the earth.

In the volcano of your infirmity
you burn your strength with the wind
transforming
the thirsty love
into the mouth of a song.)

The following poem also refers to the difficult situation in the land
of her birth – a country engulfed in hatred, mistrust and destruction.

* * *

Da li si ikada video da drvo plače
Kad mu neko lomi grane,
I čuo da cvili pod udarcem vetra
Dok ga povija na sve četiri strane?

Da li si čuo galeba kad skiči
Dok bespomoćno luta u buri,
Tražeći svoje skriveno gnezdo
U kome se guja kupa u krvi

(***
Have you ever heard a tree cry
When its branches are torn,
And heard its wailing under the blows of the wind
Twisting it in all four directions of the world?

Have you heard the sea gull screeching
While helplessly drifting into the storm,
Looking for its hidden nest
In which the serpent bathes in blood?)[24]

Vukić's poem 'Majke' ('Mothers'), dedicated to mothers everywhere, presents a moving tribute to the nurturing power of caring and
motherhood in general. These feelings of gratitude and recognition are
permeated with sadness for the many missed moments of togetherness.
There is also a feeling of guilt for not being able to rectify the situation
and offer a helping hand if needed.

One, tako duge ruke imaju
da ih oko celog sveta sviju –
da kroz stene probije njima,
i razdvoji more sinje ...
Sve oblake crne, daleke rastera,
da sunce svuda i svaki dom zagreje,
a deci našoj, i ovoga sveta,
brižna i tužna lica nasmeje ...

Tu moć poseduju i njihove sene,
da nam sigurnost i utehu pruže,
to mogu samo – one majke, žene –
od trnja života, da stvaraju ruže ...

Pa opet tako, sitne su i male
kad pate i bol grudi im razdire,
nečujno nestaju – bez pompe i slave,
i u večnom miru, nose isto ime!

Tu i tamo, neko ih spomene,
obidje im grob i spomenik siv ...
i drhtavom rukom zapali im sveću –
da savesti svojoj povrati mir ...!

(They have such long hands
able to embrace the whole world –
to blast the rocks,
and divide the blue sea.

To chase far away the dark clouds,
to warm with the sun all the homes,
and to brighten all children's sad and worried faces.

This power has even her shadow
to bring security and consolation
only mothers and women
can turn the thorns of life and roses.

And still they are small and lithe
when suffering, the pain tears their chest
they disappear gently without pomp and glory
recognized by their very name through eternity!

Every now and then someone mentions them
visiting their grave and funeral marker
lighting a candle with a trembling hand
to regain peace for the troubled conscience.) [25]

   The poems by Gavrilović, Miličić, Miladinović and Vukić presented
here point to a remarkable depth of thought and poetic eloquence,
while illuminating the experiences and tribulations of many individuals
living and working in diaspora. It is hoped that this study will help to
introduce their poetic messages to a broader reading public around the
world.

Notes

All four poetesses have graciously provided me with their poems, whether published or unpublished, in Serbian or in English translations, and have granted permission to reproduce them here. I gratefully acknowledge their co-operation and friendship. – J. M.-D.

1. *Glasnik srpskog istorijskog drustva 'Njegoš'*, published in Chicago.
2. Vasa Mihailović (ed.), *Antologija zagranične srpske poezije* (Chicago, 1988).
3. Kosara Gavrilović, *Walls and Cracks in Walls*, edited by Soza Gavrisheff (Washington, DC, 1993), p. 36.
4. *Walls...*, IV, p. 5.
5. *Walls...*, VI, p. 7.
6. Letter to the present author, 25 May 1995.
7. *Walls...*, VII, p. 8.
8. Gavrilović is referring here to Wilde's 'The Ballad of Reading Gaol', written in 1898 after his sentence to imprisonment.
9. Gavrilović's letter to the present author 25 May 1995.
10. The Serbian version of this poem was published in *Walls*Ḙ..., p. 28. Gavrilović furnished her English translation of the poem in a slightly altered form for the Serbian version 20–25 May 1995.
11. Vasa Mihailović (ed.), *U tudjem pristaništu* (Chicago, 1988).
12. Milena Miličić, *Poems – Pesme*.1990, XV, p. 73.
13. Written in 1993, unpublished.
14. *Poems – Pesme*, p. 18.
15. Written in 1993, unpublished.
16. Milica Miladinović, *Posmatranja i iskustva* (Melbourne: Srpska misao, 1968); *Satirom Svome Srpstvu Služim* (Chicago, 1991); *Basne* (Melbourne: Srpski kulturni klub 'Sv. Sava' Australia, 1972).
17. Milica Miladinović, *Satirom Svome Srpstvu Služim*, p. 55; English translation by Jelena Milojković-Djurić.
18. Milica Miladinović, *Posmatranja i iskustva*, p. 136. English translation by Jelena Milojković-Djurić.
19. Ibid., p. 138.
20. *Posmatranja i iskustva*, pp. 36–7.
21. 'Preface', *Predeli sna* (Frankfurt/Main: Jugoslovenska književna radionica, 1989), pp. 13–49.
22. Ljiljana Vukić, *Pupoljak na dlanu* (Gornji Milanovac: Dečje novine, 1995).
23. Ljiljana Vukić, *Strela Predaka* (Belgrade: Mladost, 1993), p. 5. English translation by Jelena Milojković-Djurić.
24. *Predeli sna*, p. 8. English translation by Jelena Milojković-Djurić.
25. Ljiljana Vukić, *Predeli Sna* (Frankfurt/Main: Jugoslovenska književna radionica, 1989), p. 48.

11 Post-modernist Culture and the War

Dubravka Oraić-Tolić

Letter to the Ambassador of the United States of America to the Republic of Croatia, Peter W. Galbraith, in connection with the second, revised edition of my poems, American Scream.

Dear Mr Ambassador,

Although we live in the era of a new epistolary literature, a culture of the letter in every sense of the word – including the literal – I could not until now have imagined that, from the most distant shore of Croatian culture, I too could address such a highly placed political and public personage as yourself, and that in connection with poetry, and what is more – my own poetry. You will be right to think that my letter concerns some kind of misfortune which I have experienced as the author of a poem, that I have perhaps said something in the poem owing to which I have already had, or fear that I shall have, some unpleasantness, and now I am asking you to help me realise my right to the freedom of poetic and thereby of any other kind of expression. Your suspicions are correct, but only in part: I will not ask you to help me realise the right to freedom of poetic speech and expression, for I have already made use of my right under specific circumstances and in a particular manner. I will ask you for something entirely different: an excuse for the manner in which I have realised my *licentia poetica*, and the fulfilment of one wish.

More than ten years ago, more exactly in 1981, the prominent Zagreb publisher Sveučilišna naklada (University Press) Liber published my poem *Urlik Amerike* (*American Scream*) in a once-off series of contemporary Croatian poets. I was the youngest in that series, in the company of all the contemporary classics: the greatest Croatian woman poet of the twentieth century, Vesna Parun; the Nestor of modern Croatian poetry, Dragutin Tadijanović; the protagonist of late modernism, Slavko Mihalić, and others. At first, it seemed as if that edition would be a cultural event of the first magnitude, and I myself hoped that my book would be more easily noticed in such a prestigious series. What happened was, in all likelihood, the only thing which could have happened. The books of the prominent Croatian poets, published together in one series, were immediately upon publication separated from the context in which they had appeared and associated with their personal poetic opuses, which were already established; my poem had nowhere to go – it remained hanging in the air. Modernist poetry, the sort we know from the middle of the nineteenth century up until the second half of the twentieth century, as it was conceived and developed by poets such as Baudelaire, Mallarmé, T.S. Eliot, Pound, Khlebnikov, Mandel'shtam, Benn, Célan, and which, finally, was described by the German literary scholar Hugo Friedrich in his famous book *The Structure of the Modern Lyric*, no longer existed, nor could it exist.

I cannot, of course, say what would have happened in some other time, under some other personal and cultural circumstances; I can say only what really did happen: I did not set off in the footsteps of Vesna Parun, whose name in that library also cast its lustre on my poem. Instead of continuing to write poetry, I began to write *about* poetry; instead of writing literature, I wrote *about* literature. The only thing I could still occupy myself with in the field of poetry was the palindrome – the ancient linguistic game in which the words in a sentence read the same way both forwards and backwards, from the right and from the left, from the East and from the West. In that magical game I then found the only possibility of poetic speech; it was, as it seemed to me then, purely objective, extra-personal speech, for it was not I speaking any longer, but rather words themselves, language itself.

You will surely ask yourself why I am writing this to you at all. What can the problems of modern lyricism and contemporary Croatian poetry have to do with you, the diplomatic representative of the most powerful nation of the present-day world in little Croatia, which was born in war and now with good will, though still uncertainly, takes steps towards peace? What do you have to do with me and my poem?

I will say right away: very little and very much. In my long-ago poem based on the traditions of the modernist lyric I played with the name of your country; it was its fundamental idea, it is found in the title of the book and on all its pages: more than once in my poetic text, consciously or unconsciously, I 'took the name of your country in vain'. Now, when after so many years I have, unexpectedly for myself, undertaken a second, revised edition, with a parallel text in Croatian and English, it seemed to me that my poem, stranded somewhere in the space of Croatian culture in the beginning of the 1980s, must be brought down to earth, that it is the middle of the 1990s, almost the very end of the twentieth century, that if I do not want it to vanish altogether I must explain it somehow to myself and also to others.

However, the circumstances in which this new form of the poem arose are so different from those in which the poem was first published that a normal commentary – which, considering my activity as a literary theorist, I could write with ease – is no longer sufficient for additional clarification; for not only had I changed, not only had literature changed, the whole culture had changed, the whole world had changed or was in the process of changing. And one of the conflagrations of those great changes was located, and is still located, precisely in the country in which I once long ago wrote the poem *American Scream* and in which you, after the great horrors of war, became the first representative of the country whose name I played with then in my poem. Faced with these facts, all the specialised or scholarly words I otherwise use to interpret literary or poetic texts suddenly fell mute, and the genres of notes, article or studies appeared as empty forms.

The sole manner for clarifying my poem was, as in ancient times, the epistolary form, and its ideal addressee was *you*. And precisely because today the important things are no longer my poem and I, but rather the fact that this poem, with its idea of America, arose in the country where today you represent the United States of America, I address you, respected Mr Galbraith, with a letter, but not as one person to another, but rather as the author of the poem of the Croatian *American Scream* to the representative of America in the homeland of that poem. As the author, I *then*, for the most part unconsciously, took the name of your country as the key word and idea of my poem. As the ambassador, you are *today* the symbol of that name in the country where that poem once came to be long ago. Therefore I ask you, respected Mr Ambassador, to understand that today I will seek the meaning of my *American Scream* at your address. You see, you had to get involved, unwillingly and unwittingly, along with your official

diplomatic duties or even those you chose personally in this wonderful region, in the poetic issues of the land of domicile of your
ambassadorship.

Allow me, then, to clarify to myself and to others, as I write
precisely to you, how it was that the poem *American Scream* came to
be in the distant 1970s and 1980s, how it came to this second, still
unrealised edition, what in my opinion that poem signified at that time,
the time of its writing, and what it seems to me it signifies or could
signify today, on the eve of the end of the twentieth century.

You will forgive me, I hope, for the intimate tone, at least inasmuch
as that is a presupposition of any letter-writing, including this kind of
open letter. If we can agree that style is the person, and literature a form
of autobiography, we need not be Freudians in order to seek many
secrets in childhood. Although I do not remember my father at all, for
all traces of him were lost after the end of the Second World War in
May 1945, I spent a very happy childhood in Slavonia, eastern Croatia,
where I was born. I was an only child and fatherless, and so my mother
and the wider family offered me more attention and love than was
customary. Mama and I waited for the first ten years for papa to return,
and when that did not happen mama began to live only so that one day
we would go to Zagreb and I would graduate from 'the highest
schools'. And precisely in that earliest childhood, while my experiences
of space were limited to a narrow triangle: Slavonski Brod (where papa
was an officer in the Home Guard and where he was seen for the last
time), the village of Andrijevci (where my grandmother and grand-
father lived) and Borovo, which today is occupied (where my mother
worked after the war, in the greatest Socialist enterprise of former
Yugoslavia, a rubber and shoe factory), three times, in three various
surroundings, I met the name and image of your country. So even then,
through those meetings and everything they could evoke in a child's
imagination, your country impressed on my consciousness an undefined
but powerful archetypal picture which long afterwards, though I have
never been to your country, or perhaps for that very reason, would
offer the key idea to my poem.

The first meeting with the word 'America' occurred in the first
grade of elementary school, in Borovo, when packages from UNRA
arrived at the school. The teacher brought in large brown bags and said
that the children who had no father should stand up. I stood up and

received a package. I remember a hard yellow cheese and 'Truman eggs' (the popular expression for the powdered eggs your country sent then as humanitarian aid). And just as I was reaching deeper into the bag in order to discover all its secrets, the teacher came back, and – the magic vanished. She took the package from my hands and said that it did not belong to me. I ran home in tears, and mama comforted me with something that should have been an explanation, which I accepted, but which I actually did not understand; namely, that my papa had not 'perished' in the war, but rather – 'vanished', and that children of this sort could not get the wonderful American packages.

The other two meetings with the name of your country occurred a few years later, when mama and I moved to my grandparents' in the village of Andrijevci, where a shop selling 'Borovo' shoes had opened. My mother asked to be transferred so that we could more easily survive those hard post-war years (the country people, in spite of the victory of the working class, were still needed for socialism, and the country people needed rubber overshoes!). No one, of course, wanted to go from the city to the village, and mama got the transfer. My world became the movies, and all the movies in Andrijevci were American! They came on Saturday and Sunday, always new ones. *Gunfight on Silver Creek*, *High Noon*, *The Silver Arrow*, *Gone with the Wind*... . Of all the characters I got to like the Indians, and of the actors – all of them, without exception. We played Indians and wrote to the actors; the mailman had his hands full, bringing around postcards with the smiling faces of Audie Murphy, Tony Curtis, Elizabeth Taylor, Ava Gardner and tossing them, to the horror of our parents and neighbours, through the opened panes of the windows, while on all sides on the dusty highway and in grassy courtyards our Indian arrows whizzed and incomprehensible nicknames echoed in the battle for the righteous Indian cause.

And finally, third, the childhood meeting with America that was perhaps the most foreboding took place in the fifth grade of primary school, when we learned in geography that the world was round, and had to make a plaster globe for our homework. Everyone wanted to make the most beautiful, the biggest and roundest globe in the world, but it wasn't easy at all; the plaster was hard to mix, and while we were adding the water it would already have hardened. We all got splattered by the white hardened mass, but we were extremely proud of our work.

We learned that it was precisely because the world was round that the great Spanish seafarer Christopher Columbus, wanting to reach India from the west when the Seljuks forbade travel by the East, unwittingly discovered America. It all got mixed up for me. I was an excellent student, but now for the first time something was unclear for me – especially with the directions in the world – and what was unclear to me seemed unjust and sad. On the one hand, I imagined the little Japanese on the other side of the world who had the same homework that we had and how for them, in Japan, America is actually in the east, while to us, in our village of Andrijevci, it was in the west. On the other hand, I was horribly sorry for Columbus that he thought he had reached India, while he had really discovered America, and that America was named after Amerigo Vespucci, who only described the new continent, and not for him, Columbus, who discovered it. I got an 'A', like the whole class, for my globe, but that could not comfort me. It seemed to me that there was some irreparable flaw and injustice in the globe and its roundness. And when we went home that day with our A's and our globes, the boys (among them was my future husband) started to play ball with the globes, and in that globe game one of the balls – one globe – hit our school friend in his big blond head, which looked so much like a white plaster globe, and after two days he died. In the village they said that he had died of meningitis, but we knew that he had died from the globe. And so my memory of the globe, which was to blame for the unjust story of Columbus, was combined with something entirely horrible: tangible, real evil.

I would not now tell you what happened to me later, for that is a long story where the common fate of the little girl and the little boy with the A's on their globes begins, and because I have already told that tale in brief in my booklet *Palindromska apokalipsa* (*The Palindromic Apocalypse*), not long ago, when this new war began and everyone in Croatia, myself included, felt the need to confess publicly. From that story I would only emphasise that I found myself together with that sometime schoolboy from the globe game, who like me had in the meantime become a university student, in Vienna in 1967, because of events surrounding the famous *Declaration on the Name and Position of the Croatian Literary Language*. Overnight I lost everything: family, friends, my homeland. From an ordinary student who had already begun translating and had published her first poems, I became an émigré with Austrian political asylum and the status of *Staatenlos*, I washed bottles in the Vößlauer Mineralwaßer factory, opened the door for patients at Doctor Kuntschik's in Mariahilfer Straße, I delivered flowers from the florist on Graben to elegant ladies and got tips from their housekeepers.

My first poetic collection was born then, full of the rhetoric of exile and with the sentimental title *Eyes without a Homeland*. In the spring of 1969, when in that same homeland they announced the A.B. Šimić Fund competition for young writers, I asked mama to come to Vienna and gave her my poems, so that she could submit them to the competition in Zagreb. I received first prize and returned – without a passport – home. In a week, to my great amazement, I received a new passport without any problem, and now I could travel to Vienna, hoping that I had once again become a normal citizen. When, in the spring of 1970, the long-distant boy from the globe game also returned home, arranging a passport through the then Yugoslav Embassy for his return, the same passports we had received were taken away the day after his return (of course, at that famous hour between four and five in the morning) for an entire 18 years. It was the same thing that had happened with the UNRA package: I received a gift that I thought belonged to me, and then that gift was irrevocably denied.

From today's perspective, when the war on the soil of Croatia and Bosnia-Hercegovina has written out and still is writing out unthinkable destruction and horrible human fates, revocation of a passport in the distant time before that war seems unworthy of mention. But all the same, it is precisely that limitation of freedom of movement, however silly and unconvincing it may sound today, that became the source of all my unrealised desires and social frustrations. During those years I had other fortunate and unfortunate experiences. Let me mention only the most cheerful example: regular lock-up at the times whenever President Tito would come for the opening of the big Zagreb autumn fair, for what was euphemistically called 'an informational conversation', at which no one would converse with me. Rather I, along with the former boy from the globe game, that is my husband, would sit in the police station until Tito left Zagreb. I remember, one year in Sesvete, the eastern Zagreb suburb where we were living then, we proof-read translations of Tolstoy's short stories during one such 'conversation', and our three-month-old daughter spent that day with our neighbour, who nursed her along with her own baby of the same age.

But nothing was so painful and offensive to me as the business with the passport. And there was no remedy here. Every year I requested a passport and every year I received the same negative answer. There was no Helsinki Watch, there was no commission for human rights. Denial of a passport became my Oedipus complex, the vital black and perhaps inspirational hole where all kinds of things became mixed up, and where, most likely, the unusual idea of a poetic game with the name of your country was born.

I can't say for sure when and why I took the name of your country for my poem's fundamental theme. I only know that the idea of playing with that name was already contained in the title, that I came up with the title just before or right at the time of the crushing of the so-called Croatian spring in 1971–72, that I wrote and rewrote the poem for ten years and that, finally, at no time and in no phase of writing did that name ever signify to me the real land of America, which you represent in my country today. America in my poem was always a symbol, a metaphor. Unfortunately I cannot say what the sense of that symbol and metaphor was, because it wasn't clear to me *then* either. While I was writing the poem it was sufficient for me to believe that I had discovered a great symbol and a great metaphor and that in the game with that symbol and that metaphor I could express myself and my fate. And I then, in my quixotic struggle to acquire a passport, brought myself to the point of pathetic belief that I had suffered a severe injustice, and that therefore I could perhaps also express some universal sense of human history and contemporary mankind by means of my personal fate through such a great symbol and metaphor. These strong feelings held me for a while longer after the publication of the book, and then they collapsed; the reviews gave the book a nice welcome, and then everything fell into oblivion.

The poem floated up from the sediments of time only ten years later. Namely, in the spring of 1991 friends informed me that the great 500th anniversary of Columbus's discovery of the New World was approaching (1492–1992), and that in that connection it might be interesting to prepare an English edition of this odd book that had arisen in Croatia on the topic of America. I had never thought about that before, and since in the meantime I had grown indifferent to the poem, as to poetry in general (perhaps just because of that), I behaved professionally. I arranged to get a translation from Sibelan Forrester, an American Slavist whom I met in the mid-1980s in Zagreb and who at that time translated a few texts from my collection on her own initiative. Since I no longer had a single copy of the poem, I checked the book out of the library, made a photocopy, and sent it to America without even looking at it. In June 1991, when the book was still on its way to the translator in your country, war broke out in my country, which had just proclaimed its independence. When the translation returned in spring of 1992, war was already devastating the neighbouring country of Bosnia-Hercegovina, which your country had just then recognised, along with mine.

In that year, 1991–92, while Sibelan (now already an American Bosnian daughter-in-law) was translating my poem in America, and war was raging in the homeland of that poem, I once again after many years of poetic silence took up a pen and wrote several texts, combined in a small cycle under the title 'The Croatian Egg. On the Eve of the 500th Anniversary of Columbus's Discovery of America, in 1991, and upon the Anniversary Itself (1492–1992)'. This was in fact a poetic commentary on the war. Now, when the translation of my poem from long ago arrived, I realised that this unexpected little cycle had emerged from the same head, that it was my head, that I had no head other than this one, that therefore I should not be either ashamed (the sensation that would overcome me at the thought of poetry after the publication of *American Scream*), or afraid (the sensation which ran through me while I was playing with palindromic language). It was the same inspiration from which *American Scream* arose. With that feeling I decided to incorporate the new cycle under number 91 of my old poem, and it entered like a key. Soon I had written a few more poetic texts, and they all easily found their place in the poem.

To make things even more extraordinary, at that time, without my willing it, another of my ancient texts came back to life, one I had considered dead – a good thing both for the text and for me. That was the palindromic poem 'Rim i mir/ili/ONO (1991)' ('Rome and the World/or/THAT, 1991'), which I started to write after the publication of *American Scream* as my sole possibility of poetic expression, probably feeling that it was precisely palindromic language, with its reading from both east and west, that was the most suitable language for expressing my deepest archetype – the name of your country. Soon my closest colleague at work, Dubravka Ugrešić, became involved in the fate of my poem, interpreting it in her own manner (you have surely read the 'Open Letter' of seven Croatian intellectuals to President Tudjman in the third issue of the prominent journal *Erasmus*, September 1993; her story about my poem is published in the same issue). And then I too, partly for that reason, and even more because of fate itself, was seized by the palindromic virus, and I began to interpret my poem myself. I won't repeat all of that now, for in the meantime I have compiled a book entitled *Književnost i sudbina* (*Literature and Fate*), which I hope will soon be published and which will perhaps include this letter as well. I would say only that then, in the spring of 1992, staring at my ancient *American Scream*, in the already forgotten Croatian original and the newly arrived English translation, I understood that this palindromic poem, just like several poems which had arisen during today's war, was in fact a part of *American Scream*, that in the first edition – this was now evident – my book in fact had been incomplete. I sensed that the whole text had been shaken, that the English edition, if there is one at all, could not be the same as the first Croatian edition. I felt that Columbus's anniversary ceased to be important as a reason for the publication of the second edition and that it became a part of its structure.

Only then, with those feelings and after such a long time, I re-read my poem, which had once meant so much to me. And – I was stunned. It seemed to me that I suddenly recognised the sense of the word America with which I had played at the time of writing, that I saw the idea which I had not seen at the time of writing.

The poem, as I saw it, was built as a linguistic and stylistic variation on the theme of one idea: the idea of modern European civilisation as the history of the liberation of mankind and of the realisation of the Absolute (these are at first glance ponderous words, but I'll clarify them at once). Namely, with the end of the Middle Ages (most often called 'gloomy' in these lands at the time of Real Socialism, that is, in the era of my youth), in which the main field of culture was religion, people resettled God into themselves, and the fundamental field of culture became History as the path of human liberation, that is 'the end of alienation' and 'the humanisation of the person' (well-known expressions from the philosophy of my youth). Paradise, which religion and its cultural field, the Middle Ages, expected after the completion of earthly history in Heaven, in the Modern Ages by the laws of rationalism and enlightenment was supposed to be realised in human history – on the Earth. In the person (let us remember only Descartes's *Cogito, ergo sum*) and in human history (Hegel opined that in his philosophy the Spirit had come to itself; that is, that history was finished and nothing important could be done or said any longer), such values as absolute freedom of the individual and the nation, absolute justice, equality, happiness, love, well-being and finally an entirely classless society were supposed to be realised. In the name of those ideas and ideals, the philosophers of the Modern Era built their conceptual structures, scientists discovered their inventions, poets sang their songs, and politicians fomented revolutions and conducted wars. Exhausted philosophical systems, outdated inventions, outsung songs, completed wars and stifled revolutions were replaced by new ideas and new ideals in whose names there arose new philosophical systems, new inventions, new poems, new wars and new revolutions, and when it was proved that the posited ideals were not realised in those still newer systems, still newer inventions and still newer songs, that their realisation could not be achieved either by revolutions or by wars, that paradise on earth often resulted in purgatory or hell, everything would begin again from the beginning.

In that model of history there was an empty place, a black hole from which it always peered out anew, in which it completed its cycles and finally in our era finished entirely. The name of that hole was: terror. And that hole in the Modern Era's history was nothing other than the dark side of that idea of absolute freedom. When Hegel, speaking of revolutionary violence in the time of the French revolution, poetically speculated on absolute freedom as 'the night in which all cows are black', that was precisely the model for our Modern Era history, the two sides of its fundamental idea. Namely, the grandeur and misfortune of our modern history was precisely in the fact that the freedom-bearer of that history was so elevated and so absolute that it could not be borne out in reality, and that for its realisation some violence was always necessary, so that along with all the good intentions of the bearers of that freedom there were always some injustices and some disillusionments. And that injustice and that disillusion, for their part, were the movers of a new cycle of that same history. Therefore all

Modern Era history was a history of polemical turns and inversions in philosophy, scholarship and art (Kant topples Leibniz, Hegel topples Kant and the like, Classicism topples the Baroque, Romanticism topples Classicism, and so on), and in reality a history of wars and revolutions.

And precisely here, in Columbus's route to India and his unwitting discovery of something he wasn't looking for, of the new continent on which your country would arise, is the fundamental archetype of our Modern Era civilisation and its modern history, just as Odysseus's travels to Ithaca were the model for the antique world and the civilisation of the Ancient Era, and Golgotha for the Middle Ages. Thus it becomes clear why America, along with the other two concepts, Columbus and India, never meant nor ever could mean geographical and historical reality to me, why they were and remained symbols, metaphors. In the beginning – that is, at the time I wrote my poem – they were altogether vague and unclear, whereas now they are clearer and more comprehensible, for which reason, respected Mr Ambassador, I write you this letter in the hope that I will also manage to explain it.

As symbols and as metaphors these concepts were part of the archetypal triangle of Columbus – the Modern Era historical trinity which stands at the origin of modern European civilisation. If, respected Mr Ambassador, it will not anger you, I would also like to show this Modern Era archetypal triangle graphically, primarily so that the readers of this unusual letter may grasp my idea more easily and so my apology for playing with the name of your country will be more simple and convincing:

Columbus is the symbol of the man of the Modern Era, the individual who has replaced religion with history, who has resettled God inside himself, he is the symbolic FATHER of our modern history; India is the symbol of the Modern Era's idea of freedom, of all the utopian goals which modern humanity and modern civilisation have set themselves and most often have not realised or have let down altogether (the SPIRIT of modern European history which in various forms is equal to the intentions and deeds of that person and that history); America is the symbol of reality which contradictorily and often unconsciously occurs on the path towards those goals and that idea (the CHILD of history so understood); and the 'scream' is the symbol of the violence and terror by which they have tried to realise the idea of freedom in reality, symbol of the birth pains of our modern history in which the father Columbus and the spirit of India always give birth to the child – America. Columbus is us, the individuals of the Modern Era, India is our dreams, ideas, ideals about absolute freedom and happiness, America is the forms of life, institutions and laws in which those dreams are realised or can be realised, and the 'scream' – that is the manner in which those ideals are realised in reality, that is the style of our modern European life and our modern history.

And so it went from Columbus's discovery of your land all the way up to the twentieth century. That archetypal triangle lived and directed our history only as long as any 'scream' which would arise in that triangle had meaning. And the meaning existed only as long as the old cycle of the triangle would end in one 'scream' and a new, supposedly 'better' cycle of the triangle would begin, in which new individuals would create new ideas, new dreams, and on the path to those new ideas would discover a new, 'better' reality, in order for everything to begin from the beginning on the endless path of liberation of humanity and human history.

A shift in this archetypal triangle came at that moment in modern history when two super-individuals appeared in our civilisation, two dark Columbuses (in Nietzsche's words, 'supermen') who wanted finally to complete that archetypal image, that endless replacement of new individuals, new ideas and new realities, entirely and thereby break it off (like Hegel, who did so in his philosophy), and so they came forward with two super-ideas: *the idea of the best of all nations and the idea of the best of all worlds.*

As you surely guess, respected Mr Ambassador, those two last Columbuses of the Modern Era were named Hitler and Stalin, and their ideas were Nazism and communism. And they, or rather their ideologies, asserted that those very ideas were the final ones, the best of all ideas; that one must at all costs make it to their Indias; that on the way to that goal, to those two Indias, all means were permitted. Thus, our century became the century of super-violence. In the name of the first idea Hitler undertook the destruction of the Jews in the Second World War; in the name of the second there arose first of all the first socialist country, the Soviet Union, in which the 'bourgeoisie' and the 'dishonourable intelligentsia' were destroyed, and then the enormous Real Socialist empire, in which the Eastern and Central European peoples were enslaved, among them my country and my people. Thus, our century discovered two continents of previously unthinkable evil: *Auschwitz* and the *Gulag Archipelago*. Your country fought against the first idea and its reality, defeating it in war; with the other idea and the other reality, after the great victory in the Second World War, it continued to coexist in a new world, divided 'into two like a sliced orange' (as the Croatian poet Slavko Mihalić would say). And the very fact that the other idea remained alive, what is more, that in the divided world after the Second World War it even developed, spreading and confirming the space of its power, concealed the sudden aging of all the great utopian ideas, and by this of the very triangle of Columbus, without which these ideas do not exist.

And what happened then? Well, the ageing of the last great idea of the Modern Era, communism, and by the same token the ageing of our archetypal triangle, continued unnoticed, and just as unnoticeably, after many more years and plenty of painful incidents (let's just remember Yugoslavia in 1948, Hungary in 1956, Poland in the 1980s), that idea finally died. With the death of that last great idea our archetypal Modern Era triangle died as well. This happened in the famous year 1968, when the Russian tanks rolled into Prague and crushed the Prague Spring (on the eastern side of the divided world) and when, perhaps precisely because of that, the leftist student rebellion dispersed (on the western side of the same divided world). Everyone felt that something great happened that year, but then no one could yet say what. And we in Croatia experienced something similar in our own way two years later, in the crushing of the Croatian Spring in 1971–72. There came a time in which no new great idea could appear, no new utopian dream, for the ideas of fascism and communism had compromised all ideas of freedom and liberation, the whole of our modern history.

In your country this was first felt at the time of the war in Vietnam. The children of fathers who had been heroes in the struggle against fascism in the Second World War no longer wished to be heroes, for there was no idea they would fight for that could justify a war. It was, as Frederic Jameson noted, the world's first post-modern war. And afterwards, that sense that there is no longer *anything to wish, anything to dream*, and so then *anything to stand for*, seized the whole of society, the whole of Western civilisation. Like a tower built of cards all the great ideas collapsed: capital ruled instead of revolutions, sex instead of ideal love, advertisements and kitsch instead of high art, instant information from the electronic media instead of metaphysical insights from deep books. There were no longer any utopian dreams, no 'Indias' which should be travelled to; there were no more great historical individuals, new 'Columbuses', either; there remained only a naked civilisational reality, the metaphor of 'America' and its monotonous 'scream', which became a habit.

And precisely then, in that advanced point of our century, when Columbus's triangle was already but secretly dead, my poetic idea arose too. Like many others on the eastern half of the globe, I felt the death of Columbus's triangle in my own life, in my fate. And only two decades later, in 1989, when that real wall that had divided two worlds fell down, everything became clear. And as far as I and my poem are concerned, Columbus's anniversary had to draw near for me to remember my poem; today's war, the first post-modern war on the soil of Europe, had to break out before I could finally understand it.

And so, respected Mr Ambassador, after everything I have told you and everything that can't be told but can be understood implicitly, I see the structure and idea of my poem in the following way. In the title itself three suppositions interwove: the concept of 'the American dream' from its everyday use, the title of Theodore Dreiser's *American Tragedy*, and the title of the poem *Howl* by Allen Ginsberg, translated into Croatian as *Urlik*. Examined from outside, the poem had 100 texts (the introductory poem + 99 = 100) on the model of Dante's *Divine Comedy*. Examined from within, it was a thematic and stylistic game resembling Queneau's *Stylistic Exercises*, but not on the theme of a small detail from everyday life (the fate of one button in a crowded tram), but on the great theme which I can only now formulate clearly: *the death of Columbus's archetypal triangle.*

The theme of Columbus's dead triangle was varied in my poem on four basic levels: (1) on the level of contemporary American and Western civilisation (motifs of abundance, jeans, television, Coca-Cola, speed, sex and the like); (2) on the level of the real socialist empire and its ideology (clichés of thought and language in communist society and Marxist philosophy); (3) on the level of intertextual patterns of the European and Croatian cultural traditions (quotations and paraphrases from Homer, the Bible, Ivan Gundulić, Tolstoy and the like); and, finally, (4) on the level of the apocalyptic collision of two worlds, the two sides of the world which defined Columbus's adventure: East and West (motifs of the 'United Atoms', 'mama-darkness' ['mama-tama'], Columbus's broken egg and the like). Hugo Friedrich defined the modern lyric in the above-mentioned book as a poetics of 'empty transcendence'. From that perspective, my poem *America Scream* was no longer a modern lyric, for there was no transcendence in it, not even an empty one. There was only the dead triangle of Columbus and its disconnected parts.

I would rather not tire you, respected Mr Ambassador, with a structural analysis of my own poem. The only thing I should still mention is the difference between the first and the second editions. Quantitatively, that difference is not great. From a total framing number of 100 texts, which because of the correspondence with Dante's text could not be changed, eleven changed. The new texts were introduced under the numbers 13, 18, 25, 37, 81, 91, 92, 93, 94, 95 and 97. However, the theme of the war to which some of them were dedicated, the very form of a palindrome (reading from west to east, or else from east to west) and the manner in which they were ordered in this new edition, provoked a qualitative change in the whole poem.

In the *first edition* the concept of European civilisation as a dialectic of the 'scream' within the metaphorical triangle of Columbus, India and America unconsciously emerged. Since that triangle was no longer living, and all its parts had become independent, the poem on the stylistic level was built on the model of the then popular Rubik's Cube – as a linguistic game of the most various perspectives which can be arranged from the given elements with infinite variety. With the palindromic apocalypse (81) and the texts on the topic of the war against

Croatia and the war against Bosnia-Hercegovina (91–95), the fundamental idea of the dialectic of the 'scream' became conscious of itself,
because by a deep ontological irony it was realised in the country where
it was first imagined. In the second edition the metaphorical games
ceased to be cheerful: the dead triangle came alive like a ghost, and
from once unconnected linguistic surfaces horrific Rubik's Cubes of the
first European post-modern 'scream' formed – war in the Balkans.

And here, respected Mr Ambassador, arises the question of the
horror of that war, which entered this second edition without my
willing it, and without which my poem of long ago would not have
been clear even to myself. That war is horrible because it is the first
European war after the death of Columbus's archetypal triangle,
because our civilisation no longer recognises, or does not wish to know,
the idea of freedom that defined all of modern history, and it has not
yet recognised a new freedom. When the small nations enslaved in the
great Real Socialist empire set forth their demands for freedom,
Western civilisation met this with indifference, and when such a
demand by the non-Serbian peoples in the Balkans provoked a war,
Western civilisation observed it calmly, in the expectation that this
unpleasant business would be quickly finished, so that it would not
have to respond to these peoples' demand for freedom at all. What
happened afterwards we know. Croatia and Bosnia-Hercegovina, the
main victims of the first post-Columbus European 'scream', are today
members of the international community, and their right to independence and freedom has been recognised. However, little or nothing has
been done in support of that right.

And the longer this war went on, the greater the destruction and the
human suffering, the more resolutions, peace plans and decisions of
European and international institutions which could not be carried out
in real life, the clearer it became that this war was deciding not only the
fate of the people exposed to it, but also the fate of Europe and the
world, the fate of our civilisation. After the death of the Modern Era's
absolute freedom, freedom is being decided once again, and the locus
of those decisions has become the Balkans, whose western limit is
formed by my country.

Symbols, as is well known, are those signs where there is a link
between the sign and the reality signified, like the link between smoke
and fire. In the first edition of *American Scream*, Columbus's whole

triangle and the name of your country were for me the smoke which rose vaguely above the waters of modern European history. And I, from the depths of my personal fate, played with that smoke. In this second edition, with the war which began in my country on the eve of Columbus's anniversary, I realised that there was fire behind that smoke and that this fire was great and horrible. I realised that it was the fire in which Columbus's triangle had disappeared, and, along with it, our modern history.

The first edition of *American Scream* is linked with my apology to you as the symbol of the real America in my country, whereas the second edition is linked with my wish.

I would request, respected Mr Ambassador, that you accept my apology for playing once, long ago, in the impenetrable fog of fate, with the smoke of Columbus's triangle, and in that connection with the name of your country. At the beginning of the Modern Era's civilisation, when Columbus's archetypal image arose, your country became for us the symbol of modern reality. Today, when the dead body of that triangle, and of our modern history as well, is being cremated in the Balkans, your country is the only actual reality which can bring that horrible burial to an end as soon as possible, and cause a new world and a new history to arise on the grave of dead modern history. How that world and that history will look, whether they will *be* at all, will depend on whether modern utopian freedom will be burned in this war in the Balkans, or the memory of any freedom at all. My wish is linked to that posthumous fire which was set in my country on the eve of the great anniversary of Columbus and which now rages in the heart of the Balkans. I wish your country to help in extinguishing this post-Columbus fire so that it does not turn into a universal fire.

Three basic tactics are possible in extinguishing the war in the Balkans: allowing those who set the fire to extinguish it in their own way and by their own means; abandoning the Balkans so that the fire will burn out sooner or later by itself; or hurrying to assist those whose cities and houses are burning in the arsonist's fire. In harmony with those three tactics there are three possible outcomes: the *victory* of the old Modern Era freedom; *forgetting* freedom; and *compassion* towards the freedom for which the post-Yugoslav and other post-totalitarian peoples long.

Serbia, or rather the remnant of Yugoslavia, is fighting for the first outcome, with the help of some European nations and of Russia. The ideal of freedom for Serbia and its Yugoslavia is the freedom of all Serbs gathered into one state. That goal is a typical Modern Era utopian idea: it is so great and so absolute that it cannot be realised without violence and terror over all those who are not Serbs. While Columbus's triangle was alive, while the idea of communism existed, the myth of Serbian national freedom was concealed behind the universalistic coat-tails of the liberation of the working class, and through it of humanity as such. After the death of that last Modern Era utopia, the Serbian myth of its own national freedom was driven out into open space. No other great idea protected it any longer. It was alone and naked. It faced the choice of being buried along with the last idea which had concealed it, or of forcing its will and thus surviving the death of its protecting idea. The only way to impose its will was by war. And it began to shoot at all the other peoples and people who could not accept that myth and that freedom, who did not want to sail for that India.

The difference between all the other great ideas of freedom from our Modern Era history and today's Serbian myth is that those ideas were alive, that they were born and died because that made sense, because people believed in the vanishing of some and the rise of other bearers of progress in history. Now, when after all we have lived through in the twentieth century no one believed in that, the Serbian myth dropped out of dead modern history. This was no longer the living idea of freedom, but rather its midnight shadow. The horror of this first post-modern European war is that Serbia did not begin it in the name of a new freedom which would be different, and better than previous ones, as was done in modern history, but in the name of the dead spirit of modern freedom, in the name of a ghost. If Serbia, by the strength of its (that is, the former communal) weaponry and with the help of its allies, managed to impose its idea of freedom, that is to empty large parts of Croatia and Bosnia-Hercegovina of all non-Serbian peoples and their culture so that then all Serbs could be united into one state in the spaces thus 'liberated', and if Western civilisation recognised the right to such a freedom, European history would continue to develop by the model of the Modern Era. But it would no longer be history, rather the shadow of history. For Milošević is no new Columbus, Great Serbia is no new India, and the United States of Serbia will never be a new America. They are ghosts on the grave of Modern Era history.

Another possible outcome is the forgetting of freedom in the Balkans, and thereby the forgetting of any kind of history. The main world organisations tend towards this scenario, the United Nations, and those European nations which have sent the most soldiers and negotiators to the Balkans. Fearing the ghost of history from the first scenario, European civilisation would rather choose no history at all. Like Odysseus, they bind themselves to the mast of indifference, and they plug the ears of the public so that they can listen and control the war in peace. The Balkans are left to their fate until the conquerors and victims change places and thus prove that they are equally culpable. If that happened, if European civilisation grew deaf to the cries for freedom of the post-Yugoslav peoples, we would no longer be able to inherit Columbus's triangle, an emptiness would appear on its grave, and we would be confronted with the end of history. That form of existence which Nietzsche called a 'wheel' would be realised, an 'eternal return of the same' would arise, our civilisation would lose the moral vertical which was offered by the idea of freedom: we would find ourselves 'beyond good and evil'. We would find ourselves outside history, in the endless pulsation of a new absolute: free capital and free information, which would no longer want to hear about any *other* besides itself, nor about any other freedom besides its own. And the one thing that would no longer interest that capital and that information in the case of such an outcome would be the Balkan *tabula rasa* with the black holes of freedom from which people and their culture were cleansed, in which the memory of freedom and conscience had died. It would be a farce of eternity on the ruins of morality.

And finally, the third outcome would be one where European civilisation recognised the freedom that is endangered in the Balkans, would feel compassion for it and stand up for it. The Modern Era idea of freedom was a *powerful, abstract utopian idea connected to time*: its realisation was expected in the future as long as any future remained unexposed as an unhappy present. The new idea of freedom which the war in the Balkans exposed was an entirely *fragile, individual post-utopian freedom connected to space:* its realisation occurs in the present through which flickers the memory recorded in that space. It is the freedom of completely concrete people and their culture, which neither wishes nor is able to threaten anyone, freedom connected to an inherited form of landscape, which neither wishes nor is able to go anywhere else, which is simply here, which need not be loved (as the advocates of modern freedom complain) but merely respected, left in peace to live. All modern wars, from the conquest of the Wild West to the Second World War, were wars for a new time, for the freedom of *the immigrant, the abstract citizen, the chosen people, the working class*, which is to be realised only in the future. This is a war against the freedom of a definite place, against exactly defined people, against *neighbours* with first and last names who lived in that place and the culture with which they filled their space.

And precisely that third possible outcome is connected to my wish. I would like, respected Mr Ambassador, your real country, which you represent in my country with such success, to help understand and thereby realise the freedom for which people from my country and its neighbour are longing. This is no longer an abstract utopian freedom in the distant future, freedom for an abstract nation or class in some universal empire, albeit the most perfect of all. It is a present, entirely concrete, small freedom with a full first and last name, freedom for entirely real people in a real city or village, in a real street and a real house, in a small state which neither is nor wishes to be an empire. *This is freedom which comes to a home address – as personal and intimate as a letter.* To understand that little fragile freedom means wanting – or at least being able – to send a letter to a definite person in a definite city, in a definite street, to a definite house address and in a definite state. For such a letter is a testimony that those people are living, that their city exists, their village and house, their culture and, as a protective frame from new or old empires, their state. That sort of little individual freedom with a full first and last name is the sole heir of the great abstract utopian freedom, the only way to extinguish this posthumous fire in the Balkans in which our Modern Era history is burning up, to remain historical beings.

Your country, respected Mr Ambassador, as you of course know better than I, has long stood to one side in this war. As the eldest child, and the inheritor of modern European history, it left its Mother Europe to handle her final Modern Era scream herself, but when that did not happen, when the scream became so horrible that it could no longer be listened to, your country decided to take part in extinguishing it. The future image of our history and civilisation will depend on how your country stands in this purely European matter, in this Balkan burial of

Columbus's triangle. If your country becomes involved in this conflict so as to put an end to the balancing of blame for this destruction, for these contemporary conquistadorial campaigns, if your country feels compassion for the simple and intimate freedom of space, if it takes the side of the people and culture from whom that freedom was taken by force, our civilisation will continue to develop according to the archetypal triangle of freedom. Columbus's triangle, which has died twice in our century, tortured by the dialectic of the scream, would finally be buried, but ghostly history or emptiness would not appear on its grave, our history would not come to an end. Instead it would be renewed in a new freedom – the real and intimate freedom of space. And as every space has already existed forever, as every space is inhabited by definite people, filled with a definite culture and surrounded by a definite nature, our history would no longer be the history of waiting for unknown worlds, a history of hope, as Ernst Bloch imagined it, but a 'celebration of memory', joy for what exists, as Nietzsche said.

I cannot answer this and similar difficult questions in this letter, respected Mr Ambassador, nor are those answers to be found in my poem. I see the future of my poem, in so far as such a thing in literature, and especially in poetry, can be spoken of at all, precisely because it leads to these and similar questions. One thing, however, remains certain. If it is true that it is precisely this war that is deciding the fate of Columbus's triangle, and thereby of our civilisation, your country, as the heir of that triangle, will become a part of our fate. What is more, it already is our fate. And that is noted in my poem.

In his pastoral play *Dubravka*, from which all the Dubravkas in Croatia get their name, including myself, the Croatian Baroque poet Ivan Gundulić sang a hymn to freedom from *Dubrovnik* in the seventeenth century. In his verses the poet praised that same freedom which today, at the end of the twentieth century, is being trampled in this war. It was the freedom of completely definite people, a completely definite city and culture – the freedom of the Republic of Dubrovnik in the period of its flowering:

> O lijepa, o draga, o slatka slobodo,
> dar, u kom sva blaga višnji nam Bog je do,
> uzroče istini od naše sve slave,
> uresu jedini od ove Dubrave. ...

(Oh beautiful, oh dear, oh sweet freedom,
gift in which God on high gave us all blessings,
you, cause of the truth from all our glory,
sole ornament of this Dubrava. ...)

The grenades that fell on Dubrovnik at the end of the twentieth century were grenades cast at that ancient freedom. And precisely because I believe in such a clear and simple thing as Gundulić's freedom, I do not doubt the freedom of my country, I do not doubt the will of your country to stand up for that freedom. For after the death of Columbus's triangle that properly addressed, small and fragile freedom is the only India that is worth sailing for, the only America that is worth discovering.

With particular respect I remain

Your D. O.-T.

In Zagreb, on the autumnal equinox, 1994.

Translated from the Croatian by Sibelan Forrester

Index